Urban Street
Design Guide

About Island Press

Since 1984, the nonprofit organization Island Press has been stimulating, shaping, and communicating ideas that are essential for solving environmental problems worldwide. With more than 800 titles in print and some 40 new releases each year, we are the nation's leading publisher on environmental issues. We identify innovative thinkers and emerging trends in the environmental field. We work with world-renowned experts and authors to develop cross-disciplinary solutions to environmental challenges.

Island Press designs and executes educational campaigns in conjunction with our authors to communicate their critical messages in print, in person, and online using the latest technologies, innovative programs, and the media. Our goal is to reach targeted audiences—scientists, policymakers, environmental advocates, urban planners, the media, and concerned citizens—with information that can be used to create the framework for long-term ecological health and human well-being.

Island Press gratefully acknowledges major support of our work by The Agua Fund, The Andrew W. Mellon Foundation, Betsy & Jesse Fink Foundation, The Bobolink Foundation, The Curtis and Edith Munson Foundation, Forrest C. and Frances H. Lattner Foundation, G.O. Forward Fund of the Saint Paul Foundation, Gordon and Betty Moore Foundation, The Kresge Foundation, The Margaret A. Cargill Foundation, The Overbrook Foundation, The S.D. Bechtel, Jr. Foundation, The Summit Charitable Foundation, Inc., V. Kann Rasmussen Foundation, The Wallace Alexander Gerbode Foundation, and other generous supporters.

The opinions expressed in this book are those of the author(s) and do not necessarily reflect the views of our supporters.

Urban Street
Design Guide

National Association of
City Transportation Officials

ISLANDPRESS
Washington | Covelo | London

National Association of City Transportation Officials

Linda Bailey
Acting Executive Director

David Vega-Barachowitz
Director, Designing Cities

The National Association of City Transportation Officials is a 501(c)(3) nonprofit association that represents large cities on transportation issues of local, regional, and national significance. NACTO views the transportation departments of major cities as effective and necessary partners in regional and national transportation efforts and promotes their interests in federal decision making. The organization facilitates the exchange of transportation ideas, insights, and best practices among large cities, while fostering a cooperative approach to key issues facing cities and metropolitan areas. As a coalition of city transportation departments, NACTO is committed to raising the state of practice for street design and transportation by building a common vision, sharing data, peer-to-peer exchange in workshops and conferences, and regular communication among member cities.

National Association of City Transportation Officials
55 Water Street, 9th Floor
New York, NY 10041
www.nacto.org

Cataloging-in-Publication Data has been applied for and may be obtained from the Library of Congress.

ISBN: 978-1-61091-494-9

Consultant Team: Nelson\Nygaard Consulting Associates, Sherwood Engineers

Design: Pure+Applied

Web: BlinkTag

NACTO Board of Directors:

New York, NY
Janette Sadik-Khan
NACTO President
Commissioner,
Department of Transportation

San Francisco, CA
Edward D. Reiskin
NACTO Vice President
Director of Transportation,
Municipal Transportation Agency

Chicago, IL
Gabriel Klein
NACTO Treasurer
Commissioner,
Department of Transportation

Phoenix, AZ
Wylie Bearup
NACTO Secretary
Director,
Street Transportation Department

Atlanta, GA
Richard Mendoza
Commissioner,
Department of Public Works

Baltimore, MD
William M. Johnson
Director
Department of Transportation

Boston, MA
Thomas J. Tinlin
Commissioner,
Transportation Department

Detroit, MI
Ron Freeland
CEO,
Department of Transportation

Houston, TX
Jeffrey Weatherford
Deputy Director of Public Works,
Public Works and Engineering Department

Los Angeles, CA
Jaime de la Vega
General Manager,
Department of Transportation

Minneapolis, MN
Jon Wertjes
Director of Traffic & Parking Services,
Department of Public Works

Philadelphia, PA
Rina Cutler
Deputy Mayor,
Mayor's Office of Transportation and Utilities

Portland, OR
Steve Novick
Commissioner,
Bureau of Transportation

Seattle, WA
Peter Hahn
Director,
Department of Transportation

Washington, DC
Terry Bellamy
Director,
Department of Transportation

Affiliate Members:
Arlington, VA
Austin, TX
Cambridge, MA
Hoboken, NJ
Indianapolis, IN
Memphis, TN
Oakland, CA
Ventura, CA

Acknowledgments
This project would not have been possible without the support and guidance of the Summit Foundation and the Rockefeller Foundation. Many thanks to Darryl Young and Nick Turner. The project team would also like to thank the members of the steering committee. Also thanks to David Miller, Heather Boyer, and Julie Marshall of Island Press.

THE SUMMIT
FOUNDATION

Rockefeller Foundation
Innovation for the Next 100 Years

Contents

Intersection Design Elements

Design Controls

Resources

Foreword

Janette Sadik-Khan

NACTO President
Commissioner of the New York City
Department of Transportation

This design guide is part of a growing movement among cities, from New York to San Francisco, and from Chicago to Houston. Together, we're working to build sustainable streets that will carry us into the 21st Century and create a new DNA for city streets.

As president of the National Association of City Transportation Officials (NACTO), I've led a group of cities engaged in creating this new set of standards for city streets. In 2011, we released the first edition of the Urban Bikeway Design Guide, and now we're releasing the Urban Street Design Guide with a much broader scope. The impulse to write a new guidebook started in individual cities, with over ten major guides written over the last few years, tailored to those individual cities. In New York City, we released a new Street Design Manual in 2009. These publications are already changing the game, pulling away from a bias toward highway designs that simply don't meet the complex needs of cities.

The Urban Street Design Guide gives an overview of the principles that cities are using to make their streets safe and inviting for people walking, shopping, parking, and driving in an urban context. These principles are about creating real spaces for people on city streets. Economic development is integrally tied into this transformation, since great streets support city businesses. And paramount to all of this is the safety of people, old and young, on our city streets.

Still, transformation can take time, and can be difficult in the built environment of a city. New York City and others have been leading the way to making these changes through a new, faster implementation process. Improvements that use low-cost materials like planters, bollards, and markings can bring enormous benefits in a short period of time. In this guide, for the first time, the recipes for doing these quick implementation projects are laid out for the cities around the country and the world who are clamoring for it.

The Urban Street Design Guide lays out the principles and vision for a new generation of city street design in a dynamic, engaging visual context both online and in print. It is a mirror of the new city street, easy to use and inviting for all.

About the Guide

Over the coming century, the challenges borne by cities and the burdens placed upon their streets will multiply in quantity and complexity. Growing urban populations will demand that their streets serve not only as corridors for the conveyance of people, goods, and services, but as front yards, parks, playgrounds, and public spaces. Streets must accommodate an ever-expanding set of needs. They must be safe, sustainable, resilient, multi-modal, and economically beneficial, all while accommodating traffic.

In response to these unprecedented demands, cities around the country are developing an innovative body of practice and expertise to design for and around the special characteristics of the urban environment. From New York's Times Square to Chicago's Wacker Drive to Spring Street in Los Angeles, a better approach to and understanding of street design is taking root in our cities.

Using the Guide

The contents of this guide have been formatted so that a reader may engage with the material in a non-linear fashion. While each section provides varying degrees of detail and information, these sections present individual topics which do not require a complete reading of the material that precedes it.

RELATION TO OTHER NATIONAL, STATE, AND LOCAL DESIGN GUIDELINES

The *Urban Street Design Guide* focuses on the design of city streets and public spaces. While other national manuals, such as AASHTO's *A Policy on Geometric Design of Highways and Streets*, provide a general discussion of street design in an urban context, the *Urban Street Design Guide* emphasizes city street design as a unique practice with its own set of design goals, parameters, and tools.

In instances where a particular sign or marking should be used, the guide highlights its specific reference to the *Manual for Uniform Traffic Control Devices* (MUTCD).

Many cities have already gone through the process of developing a local street design manual in the interest of creating internal design consensus between different local agencies. NACTO references materials from a selection of these guides and urges municipalities to use the *Urban Street Design Guide* as a basis for the creation of local standards.

It is important to note that urban situations are complex. The treatments and topics discussed in this guide must be tailored to individual situations and contexts. NACTO encourages good engineering judgment in all cases. Decisions should be thoroughly documented. To assist with this, this guide links to references and cites relevant materials and studies.

LEVELS OF GUIDANCE

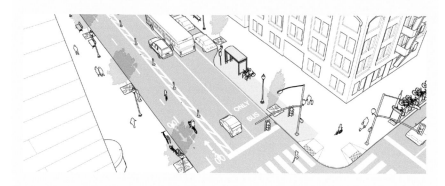

For most topics and treatments in this guide, the reader will find three levels of guidance.

Critical Features are elements for which there is a strong consensus of absolute necessity.

Recommended Features are elements for which there is a strong consensus of added value.

Optional Features are elements that may vary across cities and may add value, depending on the situation.

Note: Certain sections contain a general discussion only and have no critical, recommended, or optional points.

(above) **Key points on renderings are highlighted in yellow. Highlights either refer to the treatment or topic being discussed or to the main thrust of the image shown.**

Certain sections of the guide reference material in its companion document, the *Urban Bikeway Design Guide* (2nd edition), which may be accessed online at c4cguide.org.

Streets

Streets are the lifeblood of our communities and the foundation of our urban economies. They make up more than 80 percent of all public space in cities and have the potential to foster business activity, serve as a front yard for residents, and provide a safe place for people to get around, whether on foot, by bicycle, car, or transit. The vitality of urban life demands a design approach sensitive to the multifaceted role streets play in our cities.

Street Design Principles

The *Urban Street Design Guide* crystallizes a new approach to street design that meets the demands of today and the challenges of tomorrow. Based on the principle that streets are public spaces for people as well as arteries for traffic and transportation, this guide foregrounds the role of the street as a catalyst for urban transformation. It cements the tactics and techniques being pioneered by the nation's foremost urban engineers and designers.

Key Principles

In an urban context, street design must meet the needs of people walking, driving, cycling, and taking transit, all in a constrained space. The best street design also adds to the value of businesses, offices, and schools located along the roadway.

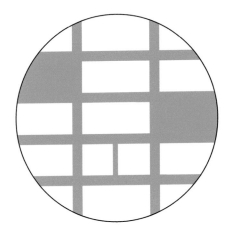

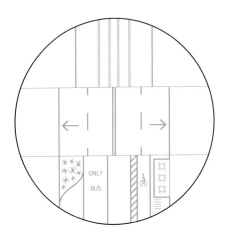

Streets Are Public Spaces
Streets are often the most vital yet underutilized public spaces in cities. In addition to providing space for travel, streets play a big role in the public life of cities and communities and should be designed as public spaces as well as channels for movement.

Great Streets are Great for Businesses
Cities have realized that streets are an economic asset as much as a functional element. Well-designed streets generate higher revenues for businesses and higher values for homeowners.[1]

Streets Can Be Changed
Transportation engineers can work flexibly within the building envelope of a street. This includes moving curbs, changing alignments, daylighting corners, and redirecting traffic where necessary. Many city streets were built or altered in a different era and need to be reconfigured to meet new needs. Street space can also be reused for different purposes, such as parklets, bike share, and traffic calming.

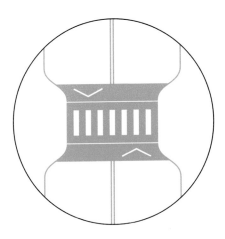

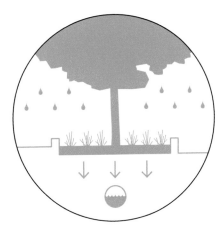

Design for Safety
In 2012 in the U.S., over 34,000 people were killed in traffic crashes, which were also the leading cause of death among children aged 5–14. These deaths and hundreds of thousands of injuries are avoidable. Traffic engineers can and should do better, by designing streets where people walking, parking, shopping, bicycling, working, and driving can cross paths safely.

Streets Are Ecosystems
Streets should be designed as ecosystems where man-made systems interface with natural systems. From pervious pavements and bioswales that manage storm-water run-off to street trees that provide shade and are critical to the health of cities, ecology has the potential to act as a driver for long-term, sustainable design.

Act Now!
Implementing projects quickly and using low-cost materials helps inform public decision making. Cities across the U.S. have begun using a phased approach to major redesigns, where interim materials are used in the short term and later replaced by permanent materials once funding is available and the public has tested the design thoroughly.

Phases of Transformation

The streets shown in this guide are depicted in three stages of transformation: existing, interim, and reconstruction.

Interim design changes for streets can be carried out using low-cost materials. These interim design strategies realize the benefits of a full reconstruction in the short term, and can help build support for projects or test their consequences. While not all projects should or need to go through these three phases, many projects can benefit from this approach.

Existing

Existing conditions demonstrate how traditional design elements, such as wide travel lanes and undifferentiated street space, have had an adverse impact on how people experience the streetscape.

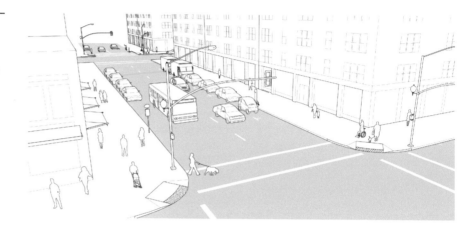

Interim Redesign

Striping and low-cost materials can realize the benefits of a full reconstruction in the short term, while allowing a city to test and adjust a proposed redesign.

Reconstruction

Full capital reconstructions can take 5–10 years. A complete upgrade might include new drainage and stormwater management provisions, raised bikeways, wider sidewalks, and traffic calming elements.

Street Design in Context

Context is a crucial, yet often overlooked, parameter in designing streets. Street design should both respond to and influence the desired character of the public realm.

Rooted in city goals and policies, designers can work to enhance their surroundings by fulfilling the visions and desires of adjacent communities through street design.

Commercial Strip

A single corridor can pass through multiple environments within the city, each with a different character and usage pattern. At right, a roadway passes through an auto-oriented commercial zone but has the same right-of-way as the two streets below.

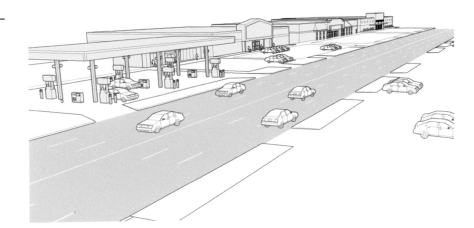

Residential Boulevard

The same right-of-way serves a different purpose as it passes through a residential area. In this environment, the street can be used for plantings, on-street parking, and shaded sidewalks.

Downtown Street

In the heart of the commercial district, the right-of-way becomes a busy, downtown space full of buses, bikes, cars, and pedestrians.

Downtown 1-Way Street

Existing

In the mid-20th century, many 2-way downtown streets were converted to 1-way operation to streamline traffic operations, reduce conflicts, and create direct access points to newly built urban freeways. Today, many of these streets operate significantly below capacity and create swaths of empty pavement in downtown areas. While many cities are converting these streets back to 2-way operation, these broad roadways can be narrowed using cycle tracks and transit lanes, which require less cost and analysis, and optimize usage of the street as a public space.

EXISTING CONDITIONS

The existing conditions shown in the illustration above are typical of many city streets in the downtown core. Many of these streets have been designed for a 15-minute peak period and remain well below capacity at other times of day.

1 Undifferentiated street space and wide travel lanes can result in higher speeds and are an ineffective use of valuable street space.

Many downtown 1-way streets have travel lanes with extra capacity or peak-hour restricted parking lanes.

Bicyclists feel uncomfortable riding between fast-moving traffic and the door zone. Double-parked vehicles may cause bicyclists to weave into traffic unpredictably, creating unsafe conditions for both motorists and bicyclists.

RECOMMENDATIONS

2 On downtown streets with heavy bus traffic, a red bus-only lane may be applied at curbside or offset. Bus-only lanes require significant enforcement and may be encroached upon by double parked cars and loading vehicles without proper enforcement. Combine bus-only lanes with bus bulbs, shelters, and transit signal priority to increase their effectiveness.

Analyze existing traffic volumes to determine whether or not peak-hour lanes can be removed and converted to on-street parking, bus or bike lanes, or additional sidewalk space. Converting underutilized travel lanes to other uses can eliminate potential conflicts within the roadway and improve traffic operations.

Reconstruction

③ A raised cycle track or parking-buffered cycle track applied on the left side of a 1-way street, removes cyclists from potential conflicts with bus traffic and creates a pedestrian safety island that decreases exposure time for pedestrians. Note: 2-way cycle tracks can also function effectively on 1-way streets in some instances. Where 2-way cycle tracks are installed, consider mitigating contra-flow turn conflicts by using bicycle signals, turn restrictions, and other means that improve visibility and slow motorists turning at the intersection.

④ As part of a full reconstruction, consider widening sidewalks, especially when they have previously been narrowed in favor of additional travel lanes.

The street illustrated above depicts a 46-foot roadway within an 86-foot right-of-way.

NEW YORK, NY

In 2010, 1st Avenue in New York City was redesigned with a 1-way cycle track, Select Bus Service, and pedestrian safety islands. The redesign not only carved out room for bicyclists, but shortened long, unsafe crossings for pedestrians. The avenue has since become a model for the successful transformation of the city's major avenues.

9

Downtown 2-Way Street

Existing

Busy downtown 2-way streets are often the most difficult streets for cities to reconfigure and retrofit. Many of these streets suffer from double parking and loading conflicts, have heavy turn volumes, and offer insufficient accommodations for bicyclists and pedestrians. Retrofit constrained 2-way streets using lane diets and conventional bike lanes or add cycle tracks that decrease the overall width and offer a higher quality bicycle facility.

EXISTING CONDITIONS

The above illustration depicts a constrained 2-way street in a central business district. While many downtown streets were converted to 1-way operations, many were not, resulting in streets that are heavily congested by buses, bikes, people, and cars. Especially in older cities, these streets may be a main route for multiple modes.

1 On major bus routes, curbside bus stops may be undermined by double-parked vehicles and heavy rush-hour traffic. These obstructions hurt the reliability and on-time performance of transit vehicles.

A lack of organization and striping can invite unintended uses and double-parking.

Freight vehicles double-parking at peak hours create weaving conflicts and safety hazards for motorists and bicyclists.

CHICAGO, IL

SAN FRANCISCO, CA

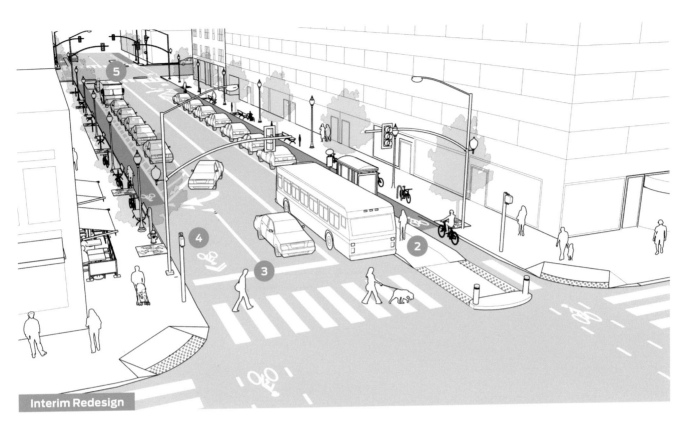

Interim Redesign

RECOMMENDATIONS

2 Bus bulbs serve as dedicated waiting areas for transit users while decreasing pedestrian exposure during crossings. Far-side placement is preferable to near-side when possible. Apply turn restrictions for near-side bus bulbs where right-turning vehicles are likely to queue in the right lane. Bus bulbs may be created in the near term without affecting drainage if slightly offset from the curb or designed as a bus-boarding island with a bicycle cut-through.

3 Create definition in the roadway using striping, cycle tracks, and narrow travel lanes.

4 Cycle tracks require special attention at intersection crossings. Conflicts should be high-lighted using intersection crossing markings with the application of color optional. Bicycle signals may need to be applied for bicycle traffic to operate safely along the corridor, though bikes may use pedestrian signals in an interim design. Turning conflicts may be reduced through the implementation of turn restrictions.

5 Restricting freight delivery or encouraging off-peak freight delivery is critical to eliminating double-parking obstructions. Off-peak deliveries are faster and more cost-efficient and avoid obstruction of the bike lane or delays to buses and local traffic. At peak loading times, dedicated loading zones should be provided to avoid the need for freight vehicles to double-park. Designers may also consider the use of wide parking lanes in these situations.[1]

The street illustrated above depicts a 50-foot roadway within an 80-foot right-of-way.

SEATTLE, WA
This street in Seattle uses a planted central median to create a street geared towards slower speeds.

Downtown Thoroughfare

Existing

Major streets that connect neighborhood centers or run through the downtown can be daunting for pedestrians to cross, depressing property values and the quality of the public realm as a result. While many of these streets have significant traffic volumes at peak hours and bustle with activity throughout the day, there are opportunities to improve these corridors for everyone using them. Add a central median and cycle tracks to enhance the experience of the street and to reduce its overall width.

EXISTING CONDITIONS

The illustration above depicts a major 2-way downtown arterial with 6–8 lanes of traffic. This street runs directly through the heart of the city and is a major connector to other neighborhoods. The street has heavy turn volumes and multiple signal phases, making it a barrier for people to cross.

Left turns are a frequent source of conflict between motorists and pedestrians and a common cause of head-on collisions.

Buses experience frequent delay due to the encroachment of parked cars, loading freight vehicles, and through traffic. Bicyclists lack any accommodation on the street whatsoever, forcing many to utilize the sidewalk as an alternative.

RECOMMENDATIONS

1 Assess left-turn volumes and evaluate the overall traffic network to determine whether or not left turns can be restricted or removed at a particular intersection. Where left turns must be retained, consider phasing options that provide a dedicated left-turn phase.

2 A parking-buffered 1-way cycle track, applied on each side of the street, offers a high-quality experience to bicyclists.

3 The cycle track may also be combined with an offset bus-boarding island and other amenities that improve operations for pedestrians and transit users.

Interim Redesign

(4) At intersections, 1-way cycle tracks may either mix with right-turning vehicles in a "mixing zone," or, where turn volumes compromise bicyclist comfort and safety, be given a dedicated bicycle phase.

As an alternative to the treatment shown above, a 6-foot pedestrian safety island and dedicated left-turn bay may be retained at the intersection by tapering the bike lane buffer and shifting the rightmost travel lane.

Many major urban arterials with commercial strip development may be reconfigured using the same principles as described above. In such cases, land use changes and access management should be coordinated with the overall vision and redesign of the street.

The street illustrated above depicts an 84-foot roadway within a 114-foot right-of-way.

BROOKLYN, NY
Striping and left-turn pocket closures provide a better pedestrian safety area.

Neighborhood Main Street

Existing

Neighborhood main streets are a nexus of neighborhood life, with high pedestrian volumes, frequent parking turnover, key transit routes, and bicyclists all vying for limited space. Main street design should limit traffic speeds and create a narrower cross-section with frequent, well-designed pedestrian crossings. In recent years, many main streets have been significantly improved through road diets and the conversion from 4 to 3 (or 6 to 5) lanes of travel with bike lanes and a center turning lane or median.

EXISTING CONDITIONS

The illustration above depicts a main street with 4 lanes of traffic. With medium traffic volumes and high pedestrian activity, the street has significant potential for regeneration as a retail district, yet currently under-performs for those who shop, eat, and walk there. Frequent destinations have resulted in multiple turning and weaving conflicts along the street.

① 4-lane configurations have been shown to increase rear-end and sideswipe vehicle crashes and pose a higher pedestrian crash risk.[1]

RECOMMENDATIONS

While road diets are not appropriate on all 4-lane cross sections, streets carrying up to 25,000 vehicles per day function effectively with 3 lanes, depending on the traffic volumes of nearby adjacent streets.[2]

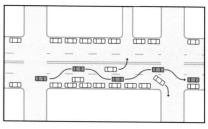

The weaving line in the 4-lane configuration shows the pattern of a driver avoiding double-parked vehicles and drivers turning left and right.

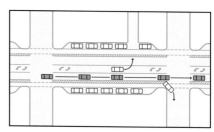

In a 3-lane configuration, the weaving and conflicts are eliminated.

Reconstruction

Road diets can improve traffic flow and reduce conflicts with turning vehicles, while increasing a road's efficiency by channeling turning vehicles out of the through lanes. Streets designed with either 2 lanes or a 2-way left-turn lane can cut crash risk by nearly half.[3]

Implementation of a road diet should consider the availability of parallel routes, the potential for mode shift, and reconfiguring signal timing and displays to improve signal operation for all users.

2 Turn lanes can help to eliminate weaving conflicts on 4-lane roads. As an alternative to the illustration above, a 6-foot pedestrian safety island can be retained in the above configuration by tapering the bike lane buffer near the intersection and shifting the through lanes to the right.

3 The application of a road diet may be carried out in two phases, the first consisting solely of striping and a center turn lane, and the second, of medians and plantings to complement the center lane.

4 From an economic standpoint, road diets often rank favorably with business owners and have a positive impact on local business activity.[4]

5 Bike boxes help cyclists make left or right turns by placing them in front of traffic at a red light. On streets with higher traffic volumes, cyclists may choose to make a two-stage turn.

6 Parklets are ideal for neighborhood main streets with active storefronts, heavy foot traffic, and lots of retail activity.

7 Streets with both heavy freight and parking demand, as well as on-street bike lanes, benefit from dedicated loading zones near the intersection. Loading zones help reduce obstruction of the bike lane and make deliveries easier for businesses. Loading zones can be striped and signed, or managed for off-peak deliveries.

The street illustrated above depicts a 64-foot roadway within a 94-foot right-of-way.

BROOKLYN, NY

Neighborhood Street

Local streets in residential neighborhoods are often underutilized as spaces for play and leisure. These streets should provide safe and inviting places to walk with direct access to local stores and schools. Design for local streets can combine stormwater management features, curb extensions, vertical speed control elements, and bicycle facilities that encourage safe speeds and meter through traffic.

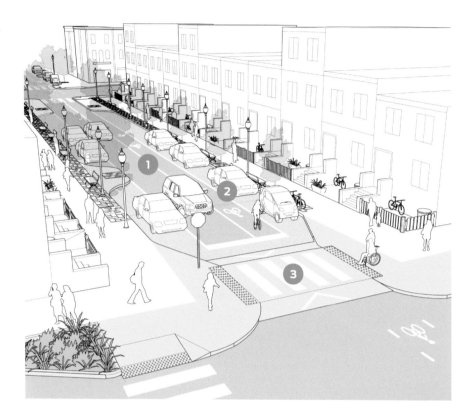

RECOMMENDATIONS

1 On 1-way neighborhood streets, travel lanes may be striped to narrow the percieved width of the roadway. An undifferentiated traveled way encourages higher speeds. Crash rates have been shown to increase as lane width increases.

2 Left-side bike lanes reduce the risk of dooring conflicts and are an effective treatment for most neighborhood streets.

3 Raised crosswalks or curb extensions maintain safe travel speeds and reinforce the residential nature of the street.[1]

The street illustrated above depicts a 30-foot roadway within a 50-foot right-of-way.

CAMBRIDGE, MA
Bike lanes narrow this residential street and serve as a valuable low-volume route for commuters.

Yield Street

2-way yield streets are appropriate in residential environments where drivers are expected to travel at low speeds. Many yield streets have significant off-street parking provisions and on-street parking utilization of 40–60% or less. Create a "checkered" parking scheme to improve the functionality of a yield street.

RECOMMENDATIONS

For a yield street to function effectively, motorists should be able to use the street intuitively without risk of head-on collision. Depending on whether the yield street has high or low parking utilization, flush curbs, or other features, its configuration may vary. A yield street with parking on both sides functions most effectively at 24–28 feet, while yield streets with parking on only one side can be as narow as 16 feet.[1]

1 All residential streets should provide safe and inviting places to walk and good access to local stores and schools. Design should mitigate the effects of driveway conflicts, reduce cut-through traffic, and maintain slow speeds conducive to traffic safety.

2 Driveways should be constructed to minimize intrusion upon the sidewalk. Maintain sidewalk materials and grade across driveways.

3 The planted furniture zone of the sidewalk creates opportunities for street trees, bioswales, pervious strips, and rain gardens.

4 While most yield streets should have a minimum of signage and striping, signage should be used to indicate bidirectional traffic at transition points or where 2-way operation has recently been introduced.

Parking utilization on yield streets should be monitored closely. Before and after conversion, cities should consult with local residents to see whether or not a "checkered" parking scheme should be striped or remain unofficial.

The street illustrated above depicts a 30-foot roadway within a 45-foot right-of-way.

PORTLAND, OR
A curb extension narrows the entry and slows turning vehicles at the mouth of this yield street.

Boulevard

Boulevards separate very large streets into parallel urban realms, buffering the commercial or residential street edge from the high-speed throughway by means of multiway operations and frontage roads. Many boulevards were built at the turn of the 20th century, but fell into disrepair or were redesigned to highway standards over the course of the century. Today, many cities are restoring these boulevards to their former grandeur or applying updated boulevard design standards to overbuilt urban arterials.

RECOMMENDATIONS

1 The frontage road, especially in a residential context, benefits from traffic calming at intersections and midblock as well as pedestrian-scale lighting and street trees. These enhancements preserve safe speeds for bicyclists and pedestrians, and encourage recreational and commercial activity.

2 Boulevards require careful attention at intersections with cross traffic. Poor design can result in intersections that are confusing or unsafe for all street users. In general, frontage roads should be stop-controlled, except in cases where volumes of cross traffic fail to provide sufficient gaps to pass. In such cases, require vehicles on the frontage road to turn or install a signal in conjunction with the through lanes.[1]

BERKELEY, CA
Frontage roads create a parallel low-speed urban environment ideal for retail activity.

3 Boulevard medians are often under-designed or inhospitable as public space. Intersection conflicts and delays undermine their use. Medians can be activated through the addition of shared use paths, seating, and recreational amenities. Consider the installation of curb extensions or midblock crossings to facilitate median use and access, or design the frontage road with a flush curb to create a seamless transition between the sidewalk, street, and median.

SAN FRANCISCO, CA
Low-speed, low-volume frontage roads are shared by multiple users.

Transit providers may prefer to use the frontage road over the throughway to reduce risks of rear-end collisions and provide more direct access to adjacent homes and businesses. When used as a transit route, the frontage road should be designed with curb extensions and/or speed cushions and should be signalized to ensure the effectiveness of transit service.

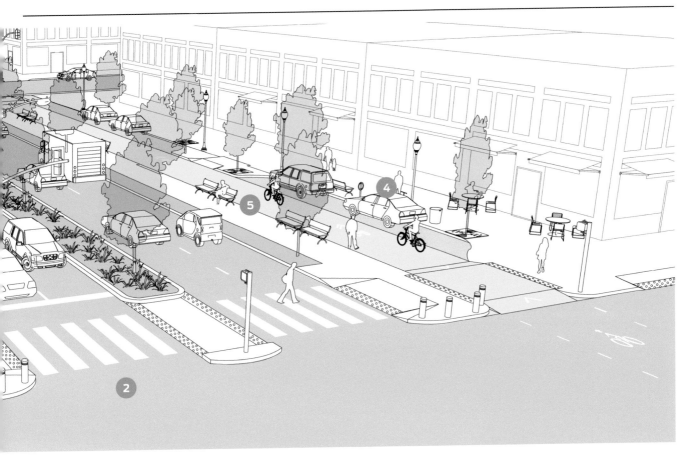

Frontage roads provide additional parking to local businesses and residents. Back-in angled parking may be an option if space is available.

Boulevards may benefit from access management strategies. At local or low-volume intersections, consider creating a T-intersection by extending the median and forcing turns. Through traffic and recreational median users both benefit from this configuration. Midblock pedestrian crossings should still be provided to preserve crossing opportunities.

5 A boulevard median with a shared use path should be designed with careful attention to intersection crossings and turning conflicts. Use access management strategies and turn requirements to eliminate these conflicts and ensure that potential intersection conflicts are well marked and highly visible to motorists turning off the throughway as well as to cross traffic.

The street illustrated above depicts a 116-foot roadway within a 164-foot right-of-way.

PHILADELPHIA, PA
Rows of trees make walking pleasant and provide shade in summer.

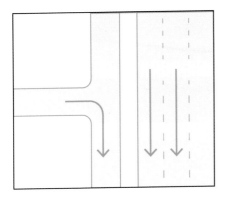

Residential Boulevard

Existing

Broad historic boulevards and parkways often function as high-speed thoroughfares, even though their adjacent land uses may be primarily residential in nature. In many cases, these streets have excess width, underutilized on-street parking, and too many travel lanes. Retrofit residential boulevards by expanding or activating the median, adding curbside or left-side bike lanes, and curb extensions that provide direct access from homes to the center median.

EXISTING CONDITIONS

The illustration above depicts a broad residential thoroughfare in an older neighborhood. The central median is underutilized. While traffic volumes may not be high, speeds are, creating highway-like conditions in a predominantly residential area.

1 Many historic central medians are underused and lack recreational space. High speed crossings make it difficult for residents and children to safely access the median.

While parkways and boulevards provide natural links in an active transportation network, many lack safe and adequate paths for recreational use.

Parking demand and utilization may vary depending on the amount of off-street parking available to residents.

BOSTON, MA
Commonwealth Avenue has a linear park in its median.

NEW YORK, NY
A cycle track takes advantage of the central median and insulates cyclists from double parking.

Reconstruction

RECOMMENDATIONS

2 Activate the central median with plantings, street trees, walkways, and seating. Broad central medians can become a community focal point as well as an active space for recreation, exercise, and leisure. Provide curb extensions and/or midblock crossings to make it safer and easier for residents to access the median.

3 A raised cycle track takes advantage of the central right-of-way, avoids frequent conflicts with driveways and double-parked cars, and effectively expands the amount of recreational space along the corridor.[1]

4 Provide curbside parking for residents. Curbside parking provides access to the recreational median for visitors, space for residents' guests to park, and narrows the overall cross-section of the road, reinforcing its residential character. Where on-street parking remains underutilized, consider adding curb extensions, bicycle corrals, or expanding the sidewalk to take advantage of the excess pavement.

The street illustrated above depicts an 80-foot roadway within a 110-foot right-of-way.

ST. LOUIS, MO
Many historic neighborhoods have medians with untapped civic potential.

Transit Corridor

Transit corridors, including light rail (LRT), streetcar, and bus rapid transit (BRT), promote economic development around high-quality transit service while fostering a pedestrian scale in which walking and biking actively complement public transit. As major generators of pedestrian traffic, heavy surface transit routes should be prioritized for pedestrian safety improvements in both the immediate surrounding area and major access routes within the transit access shed. When redesigning streets for high-quality transit service, designers should assess how transit service is impacted not only by the geometry of the corridor, but also its existing signal timing, signal phasing, turns, and other operations that may jeopardize the quality of service.

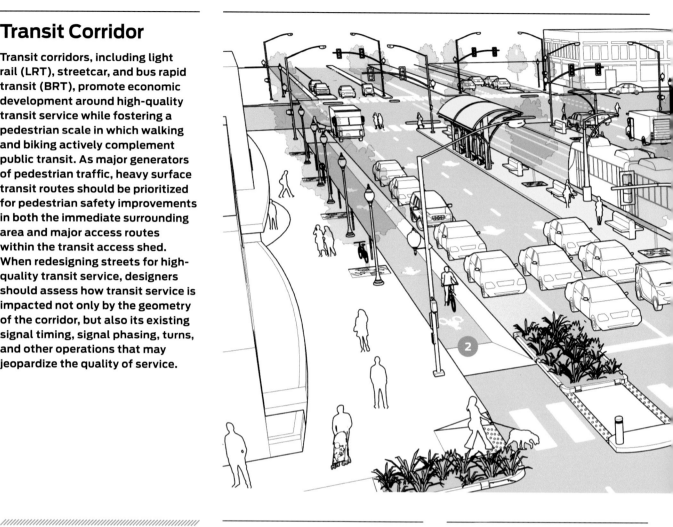

RECOMMENDATIONS

1 Transit corridor retrofits should be coordinated with land use changes to maximize a corridor's potential for economic growth and physical transformation. Setback guidelines and other land use regulations should be tailored to create a pedestrian-scale environment.[1]

2 A raised cycle track on both sides of the corridor promotes the combination of bicycle and transit usage. A center-running 1-way or 2-way cycle track may be preferable in some cases to reduce the dangers of turning conflicts in combination with transit.

Enforcement measures should be put in place to discourage encroaching vehicles from using the dedicated bus lanes. In some cases, median transit lanes may serve as a route for emergency vehicles.

3 Corridors with high transit traffic, where double-parking and local traffic pose obstacles to effective transit, should be considered for BRT, LRT, or streetcar. High-quality transit service and median transit lanes decrease conflicts between buses and through traffic on heavy transit routes, can speed travel times, and reinforce the desirability of transit as an option.[2]

Wide transit corridors are challenging to cross in a single cycle. Consider the tradeoffs between shortening signal cycle lengths and providing sufficient time for all pedestrians to cross the street.

4 Off-board fare collection speeds up transit vehicles and reduces wait time for passengers.

Transit signal priority gives buses and light rail more green time and should always be used as part of BRT or LRT operations.[3]

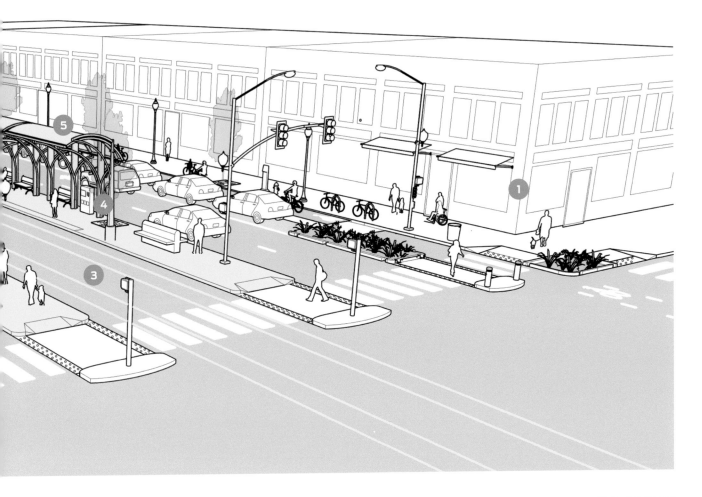

PHOENIX, AZ

Light rail expansions should be coordinated with land use changes to promote development of the corridor.

A side-running bus, streetcar, or light rail system may be preferable when adjacent land uses are heavily weighted toward one side of the corridor.

5 The design of a transit stop is an opportunity to reinforce the speed and desirability of the system. Shelters and stations should be built to accommodate the typical number of waiting passengers at the peak hour.

Loading zones should be provided near the intersection in the floating parking lane to discourage double parking.

The street illustrated above depicts a 120-foot roadway within a 150-foot right-of-way.

Green Alley

The majority of residential alleys have low traffic and infrequent repaving cycles, resulting in back roads with potholes and puddling that are uninviting or unattractive. Green alleys use sustainable materials, pervious pavements, and effective drainage to create an inviting public space for people to walk, play, and interact.[1]

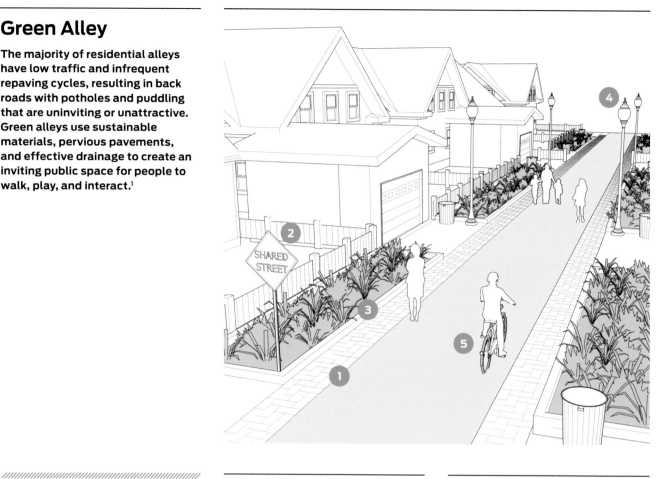

RECOMMENDATIONS

1 Construct green alleys with low-impact pavement materials, such as pervious pavements with high reflectivity to reduce heat island effects.

DETROIT, MI
This alley in Detroit was transformed to manage stormwater using pervious pavement and native plants along the walkway.

2 Alleys may be operated as pedestrian-only environments or as shared streets. Use bollards, signs, and design features that make clear the intended alley users.

Alley greening and maintenance may be initiated and carried out by local residents or neighborhood associations.[2]

3 To avoid puddling, stormwater run-off should be infiltrated in-place using permeable paving or rain gardens at the edge of the pedestrian path.[3]

4 To maintain a safe environment, green alleys should have adequate lighting. Pedestrian-scale light fixtures that focus their illumination toward the ground and minimize light pollution are recommended. Public safety is of paramount consideration for all new and existing alleys. Good lighting is an essential prerequisite to a feeling of public safety in alleys.

5 Green alleys often run parallel to the larger street network, making them ideal low-speed, low-volume links for cyclists.

Alleys provide direct property access and eliminate the need for driveways along main roads where people are walking and biking. Consider the use of alleys in all new developments and renovations to existing properties.[4]

Green alleys may present certain unconventional maintenance responsibilities. Use of textured pavements and other materials may be challenging to existing street sweepers and snowplows. Similar to shared streets, alleys may benefit from the application of snowplow compatible materials and provisions for maintenance equipment access.

The alley shown above depicts a 14-foot path within a 28-foot right-of-way.

Commercial Alley

Commercial alleys, though often thought of as dirty or unsafe, can be designed to play an integral role in a downtown street network and improve the pedestrian realm in and around commercial areas. The design of commercial alleys should strive to balance their necessary utilitarian features with their place-making potential.

RECOMMENDATIONS

Intersections between alleys and sidewalks have the potential to obstruct visibility for vehicles (if permitted) and passing pedestrians. Raise the intersection to the sidewalk grade and add rumble strips to mitigate these visibility issues. Warning signs should be provided to warn pedestrians of encroaching traffic.[1]

Freight may use green alleys for loading and unloading, which reduces double-parking on neighborhood streets.

1 Where access for vehicles is prohibited or minimal, commercial alleys may be constructed using low-impact pavement materials, such as pervious or modular paving.

2 Bicycle traffic may use commercial alleys. Similar regulations to those of shared space should apply.

Commercial alleys can be restricted for traffic during non-delivery hours for outdoor seating or other uses.

Where vehicle access is permitted, alleys should be maintained to allow easy access by trucks and other freight vehicles. Bollards and other street furniture should be designed to minimize conflicts with freight movements. In some cases, freight may be conveyed using hand trucks or small vehicles. In these cases, careful attention should be paid to the location of curbs and the access from loading zones to entrances to ensure smooth deliveries.

The alley shown above depicts a 10-foot wide path within a 20-foot right-of-way.

SAN FRANCISCO, CA
Alley redesign can feature pavers for the traveled way, parking restrictions, and additional public space.

Residential Shared Street

Existing

Low-volume residential streets, especially in older cities, often have narrow or crumbling sidewalks. Many of these streets operate as de facto shared spaces in which children play and people walk, sharing the roadway with drivers. Depending on their volume and role in the traffic network, these streets have the potential to be redesigned and enhanced as shared streets. Shared streets can meet the desires of adjacent residents and function foremost as a public space for recreation, socializing, and leisure. It is important to note that while many low-volume residential streets were designed without sidewalks and may function as shared streets, shared street conversions necessitate a deliberate redesign rather than the addition of regulatory signage alone. Sidewalks should be added when upgrading substandard neighborhood streets.

EXISTING CONDITIONS

The residential street in the illustration above is common in neighborhoods with low traffic volumes. Here the configuration of the street network has formed a street segment that functions naturally as a space for children to play and for residents as a gathering place.

Many low-volume residential streets in the United States were designed without sidewalks. Most of these streets have limited access and low volumes, allowing them to operate informally as shared spaces. Cities should aim to maintain low speeds and volumes on these streets, reinforcing their shared nature through materials and targeted design enhancements.

RECOMMENDATIONS

1. Textured or pervious pavements that are flush with the curb reinforce the pedestrian-priority nature of the street. Special pavements,

especially unit pavers, may be subject to additional maintenance costs and should be selected based on regional climate and long-term durability. Selection of snowplow-compatible materials is recommended for colder climates. Drainage channels should be provided either at the center of the street or along the flush curb, depending on underground utilities and other existing conditions.

2. Street furniture, including bollards, benches, planters, and bicycle parking, can help define a shared space, subtly delineating the traveled way from the pedestrian-only space.[1]

3. A shared street sign should be used at the entrance to a shared street. In some cases, a modified YIELD TO PEDESTRIANS sign (MUTCD 2B-2) may be added to reinforce the conversion in early stages.

Provide tactile warning strips at the entrance to all shared spaces. Warning strips should alert drivers and pedestrians.[2]

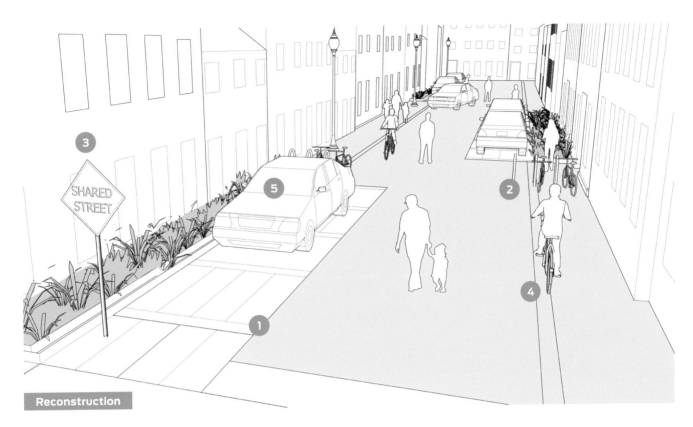

Reconstruction

④ Shared streets generally permit motorists and bicyclists to operate in a 2-way fashion. Narrower shared streets may be made 1-way for motorists, though 2-way bicycle traffic should still be permitted. Certain restrictions and regulations may apply to vehicles on a shared street. Designers should strive to make these behaviors implicit through the design details of the street itself.

⑤ On wider shared streets, staggered blocks of landscaping, head-in parking, back-in angled parking, or perpendicular parking can be used to create a chicane effect.[3] In some cases, parking may be permitted directly adjacent to properties in a residential environment. Bollards, paving materials, and street furniture help to define parking spaces and to delineate private from public space.

Where necessary, traffic volumes can be decreased through network design and traffic calming as part of a conversion.

SANTA MONICA, CA
Signage reinforces the transition to a shared street.

Depending on right-of-way, designers may consider providing a 3–5-foot clear path, protected from traffic. The clear path may be defined using planters, bollards, and street furniture, as well as detectable warning strips or textured pavers. For narrower shared streets and alleys, use of a clear path is discouraged.

The street illustrated above depicts a 20-foot shared way within a 30-foot right-of-way.

VICTORIA, BC, CANADA
Angled parking in alternating swaths curves the path of travel.

Commercial Shared Street

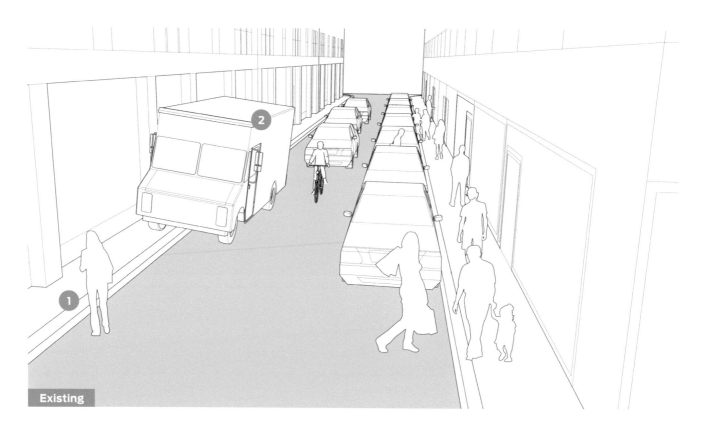

Existing

Many narrow or crowded down-town streets operate informally as shared streets during rush hour or at lunchtime, but are not regulated as such. A commercial shared street environment should be considered in places where pedestrian activity is high and vehicle volumes are either low or discouraged. Commercial shared streets can be designed for narrow or wide cross sections, but become increasingly complex and difficult to maintain as a shared space as width increases.

From 1960–80, many neighborhood main streets and downtown retail corridors were converted to pedestrian-only usage. These conversions were often called "pedestrian malls." In an era of declining downtown retail revenues due to competition from shopping center developments outside of historic cores, many of these conversions were unsuccessful or suffered from poor maintenance and a lack of programming or policing.[1]

Commercial shared streets differ from this earlier generation of pedestrian malls in both their regulation and implementation. Shared streets maintain access for vehicles operating at low speeds and are designed to permit easy loading and unloading for trucks at designated hours. They are designed to implicitly slow traffic speeds using pedestrian volumes, design, and other cues to slow or divert traffic.

EXISTING CONDITIONS

The street in the rendering above is a common sight in many older cities where downtown commercial streets may predate wider grid streets. In newer cities, a retail district with heavy parking utilization and narrow, congested sidewalks may have similar conditions or opportunities.

1 Sidewalk congestion creates unsafe conditions, as crowding forces some pedestrians to walk in the street to avoid crowds.

Vehicles in search of on-street parking create traffic congestion.

2 Loading and unloading trucks obstruct pedestrian and vehicle traffic. Truck drivers park on the side-walk to preserve vehicle flow while unloading, forcing pedestrians to mix with motorists.

RECOMMENDATIONS

3 Textured or pervious pavements that are flush with the curb reinforce the pedestrian-priority operation of the street and delineate a non-linear path of travel or narrow carriageway. Special pavements, especially unit pavers, may be subject to additional maintenance costs and should be selected based on regional climate and long-term durability. Selection of snowplow-compatible materials is recommended for colder climates. Drainage channels should be provided either at the center of the street or along the flush curb, depending on existing conditions and

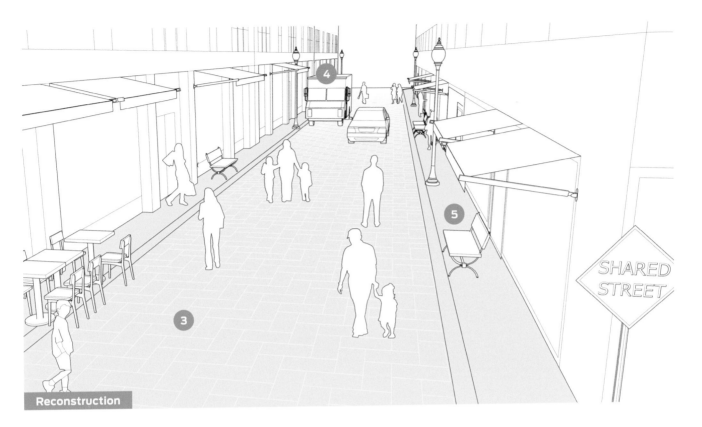

Reconstruction

the overall street width. Drainage channels are often used to define the traveled way from the clear path.[2]

MONTREAL, CANADA
Shared streets should be designed so that people walk comfortably and naturally within the roadway.

④ Commercial shared streets should be accessible by single-unit trucks making deliveries. Where commercial alleys are non-existent, it may be advantageous to design a shared street to accommodate large trucks, though significant changes to the design should be avoided. Designated loading and unloading zones may be defined through differences in pavement pattern or use of striping and signage.

⑤ Street furniture, including bollards, benches, planters, street lights, sculptures, trees, and bicycle parking, may be sited to provide definition for a shared space, subtly delineating the traveled way from the pedestrian-exclusive area.

Shared streets may be closed to through traffic for specific portions of the day. Use movable planters and time-of-day restrictions to regulate the shared space.

Provide tactile warning strips at the entrance to all shared spaces. Warning strips should span the entire intersection crossing.

Prior to the application of a shared street, cities are encouraged to experiment with car-free hours or to test a conversion using temporary materials to evaluate the potential impact on traffic operations.

Commercial shared streets restrict transit access. For pedestrian streets that provide direct transit access, consider the application of a transit mall.[3]

CAMBRIDGE, MA
Street furniture helps define the shared space.

Depending on the overall street width, designers may consider providing a 3–5-foot-clear path protected from traffic. The clear path should be defined using planters, bollards, and street furniture, as well as detectable warning strips or textured pavers. For narrower shared streets and alleys, use of a clear path is discouraged.

The street illustrated above depicts a 22-foot shared way within a 30-foot right-of-way.

CAMBRIDGE SHARED STREETS

The City of Cambridge converted Harvard Square's Winthrop Street into a shared street in 2007. This conversion was followed by the conversion of an alley, Palmer Street, into another shared corridor. Prior to their conversion, both streets were cramped and poorly maintained. Winthrop Street had narrow sidewalks and uneven pavers that created an inhospitable environment for pedestrians. Both streets failed to meet accessibility standards of the Americans with Disabilities Act. With vehicle volumes under 1,000 ADT and high pedestrian traffic, the street already implicitly functioned as a shared street.

The city's project formalized the shared operation of the corridor, while the reconstruction allowed for more efficient use of space on a small street and enabled the city to accommodate pedestrians, bicyclists, outdoor diners, and motorists using a flush curb. Shared streets in Cambridge have transformed the public space, integrating and balancing commercial uses, streetperformers, restaurant activity, and transportation using an aesthetically pleasing design.

Interagency Coordination
Multiple government departments worked collaboratively to realize Cambridge's shared streets. The Community Development Department managed the design process and community involvement through a citizen advisory committee. Public Works reviewed the project design regarding long-term maintenance and accessibility issues. The Traffic, Parking, and Transportation Department oversaw traffic and parking regulations, ensuring that deliveries were still feasible. Champions at the Harvard Square Business Association, the Harvard Square Design Committee, and the Historic Commission have also contributed to the success of the shared streets. As part of these efforts, the city also created a new categorization for shared streets within their city code.

Maintenance
Both Winthrop and Palmer Street use standard color and interlocking concrete pavers, which facilitate easy maintenance. On Palmer Street, the use of in-ground lighting has proven more challenging to maintain. Similarly, bollards installed to protect buildings on Palmer Street have suffered wear and tear from truck traffic.

Snow Removal and Stormwater Management
In Cambridge, property owners are responsible for removing snow from sidewalks, while the vity removes snow from the street. After conversion to a shared street, these delineations proved less stark. In Harvard Square, property owners have proactively shouldered additional snow removal responsibilities. Stormwater management has also been a consideration, because removing a curb changes runoff flows. To prevent puddling near buildings, shared streets in Cambridge grade toward a small gully in the center of the road.

Street Design Elements

The elements that make up city streets, from sidewalks to travel lanes to transit stops, all vie for space within a limited right-of-way. Transportation planners and engineers can use this toolbox to optimize the benefits the community receives from its streets.

Lane Width

The width allocated to lanes for motorists, buses, trucks, bikes, and parked cars is a sensitive and crucial aspect of street design. Lane widths should be considered within the assemblage of a given street delineating space to serve all needs, including travel lanes, safety islands, bike lanes, and sidewalks. Each lane width discussion should be informed by an understanding of the goals for traffic calming as well as making adequate space for larger vehicles, such as trucks and buses.

Existing

12' 12' 12' 12'

Travel lanes are striped to define the intended path of travel for vehicles along a corridor. Historically, wider travel lanes (11–13 feet) have been favored to create a more forgiving buffer to drivers, especially in high-speed environments where narrow lanes may feel uncomfortable or increase potential for side-swipe collisions.

Lane widths less than 12 feet have also historically been assumed to decrease traffic flow and capacity, a claim new research refutes.[1]

DISCUSSION

The relationship between lane widths and vehicle speed is complicated by many factors, including time of day, the amount of traffic present, and even the age of the driver. Narrower streets help promote slower driving speeds. which in turn reduce the severity of crashes. Narrower streets have other benefits as well, including reduced crossing distances, shorter signal cycles, less stormwater, and less construction material to build.

Lane widths of 10 feet are appropriate in urban areas and have a positive impact on a street's safety without impacting traffic operations. For designated truck or transit routes, one travel lane of 11 feet may be used in each direction. In select cases, narrower travel lanes (9–9.5 feet) can be effective as through lanes in conjunction with a turn lane.[2]

RECOMMENDED

Lanes greater than 11 feet should not be used as they may cause unintended speeding and assume valuable right-of-way at the expense of other modes.

Restrictive policies that favor the use of wider travel lanes have no place in constrained urban settings, where every foot counts. Research has shown that narrower lane widths can effectively manage speeds without decreasing safety and that wider lanes do not correlate to safer streets.[3] Moreover, wider travel lanes also increase exposure and crossing distance for pedestrians at intersections and midblock crossings.[4]

Use striping to channelize traffic, demarcate the road for other uses, and minimize lane width.

SAN FRANCISCO, CA
Striping should be used to delineate parking and curbside uses from the travel lane.

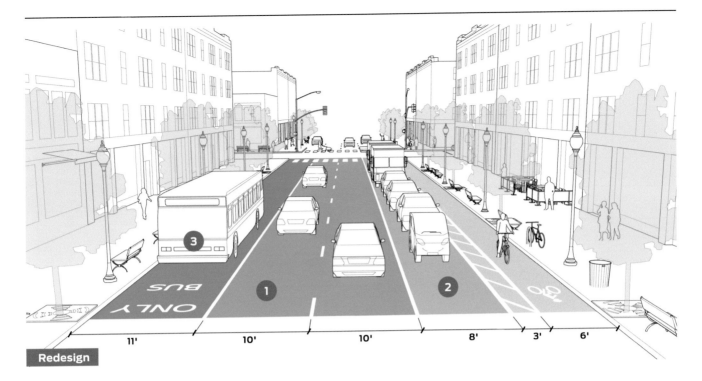

Redesign

11'   10'   10'   8'   3'   6'

① Lane width should be considered within the overall assemblage of the street. Travel lane widths of 10 feet generally provide adequate safety in urban settings while discouraging speeding. Cities may choose to use 11-foot lanes on designated truck and bus routes (one 11-foot lane per direction) or adjacent to lanes in the opposing direction.

Additional lane width may also be necessary for receiving lanes at turning locations with tight curves, as vehicles take up more horizontal space at a curve than a straightaway.

Wide lanes and offsets to medians are not required but may be beneficial and necessary from a safety point of view.

OPTIONAL

② Parking lane widths of 7–9 feet are generally recommended. Cities are encouraged to demarcate the parking lane to indicate to drivers how close they are to parked cars. In certain cases, especially where loading and double parking are present, wide parking lanes (up to 15 feet) may be used. Wide parking lanes can serve multiple functions, including as industrial loading zones or as an interim space for bicyclists.

③ For multi-lane roadways where transit or freight vehicles are present and require a wider travel lane, the wider lane should be the outside lane (curbside or next to parking). Inside lanes should continue to be designed at the minimum possible width. Major truck or transit routes through urban areas may require the use of wider lane widths.

2-way streets with low or medium volumes of traffic may benefit from the use of a dashed center line with narrow lane widths or no center line at all. In such instances, a city may be able to allocate additional right-of-way to bicyclists or pedestrians, while permitting motorists to cross the center of the roadway when passing.

Wider travel lanes are correlated with higher vehicle speeds.

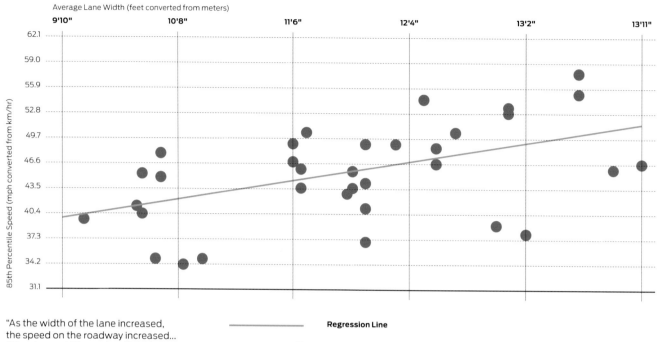

"As the width of the lane increased, the speed on the roadway increased... When lane widths are 1 m (3.3 ft) greater, speeds are predicted to be 15 km/h (9.4 mph) faster."

Chart source: Fitzpatrick, Kay, Paul Carlson, Marcus Brewer, and Mark Wooldridge. 2000. "Design Factors That Affect Driver Speed on Suburban Streets." *Transportation Research Record* 1751: 18–25.

Regression Line

85th Percentile Speed of Traffic

Sidewalks

Sidewalks play a vital role in city life. As conduits for pedestrian movement and access, they enhance connectivity and promote walking. As public spaces, sidewalks serve as the front steps to the city, activating streets socially and economically. Safe, accessible, and well-maintained sidewalks are a fundamental and necessary investment for cities, and have been found to enhance general public health and maximize social capital. Just as roadway expansions and improvements have historically enhanced travel for motorists, superior sidewalk design can encourage walking by making it more attractive.

Sidewalk Zones

Prevailing design guidelines recommend a minimum sidewalk cross-section of 5 feet, exclusive of other amenities and large enough for two people walking side by side. While this dimension meets minimum ADA accessibility standards, many cities have chosen to adopt wider standards. Sidewalk standards should accommodate higher anticipated pedestrian volumes and provide ample space for an expanded frontage zone as well as other street furniture, such as trash receptacles, bus stops, signage, and bike share stations.[1]

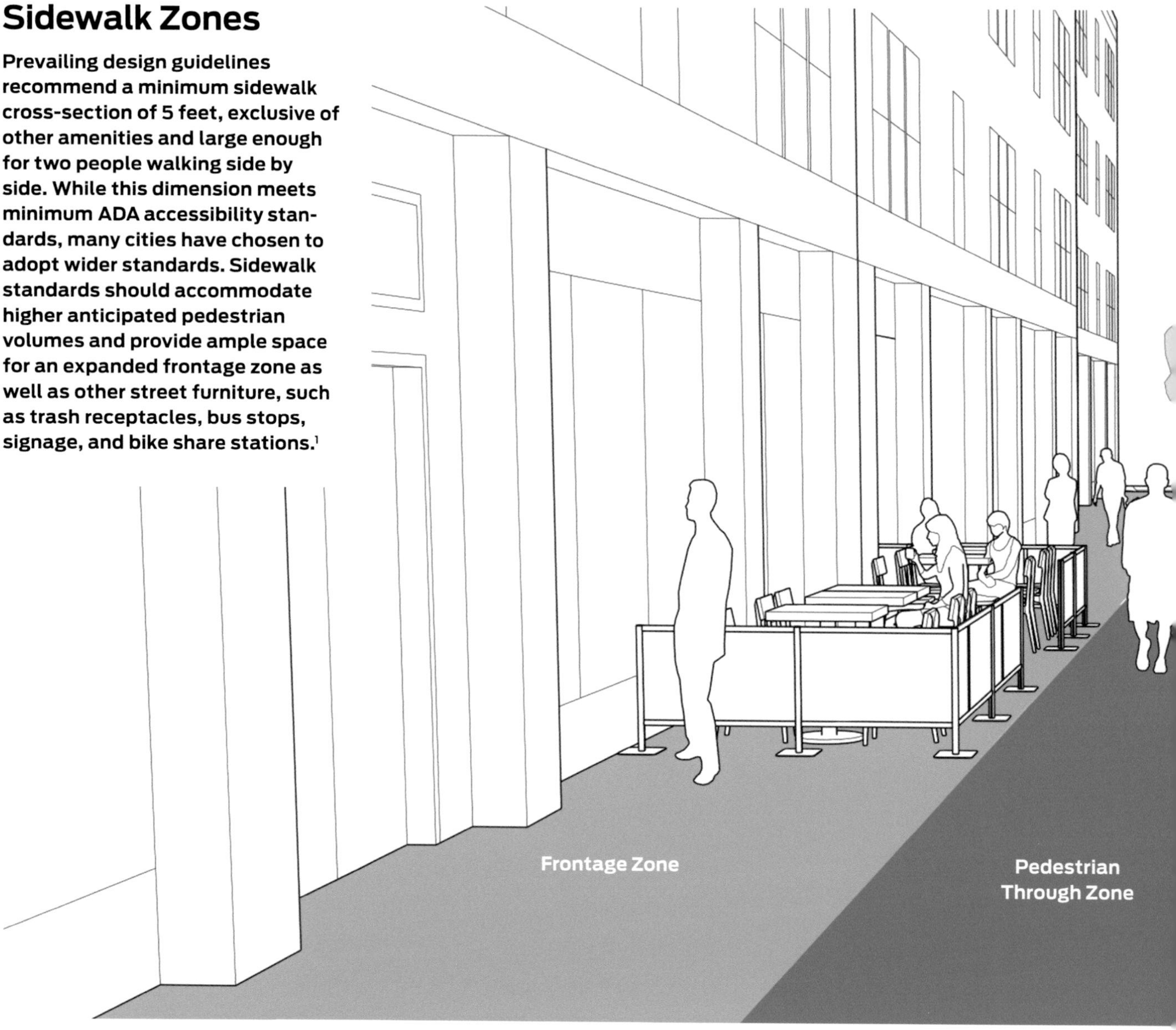

Frontage Zone

Pedestrian Through Zone

1 FRONTAGE ZONE

The frontage zone describes the section of the sidewalk that functions as an extension of the building, whether through entryways and doors or sidewalk cafes and sandwich boards. The frontage zone consists of both the structure and the façade of the building fronting the street, as well as the space immediately adjacent to the building.

2 PEDESTRIAN THROUGH ZONE

The pedestrian through zone is the primary, accessible pathway that runs parallel to the street. The through zone ensures that pedestrians have a safe and adequate place to walk and should be 5–7 feet wide in residential settings and 8–12 feet wide in downtown or commercial areas.

Street Furniture/
Curb Zone

Enhancement/
Buffer Zone

 **3 STREET FURNITURE/
CURB ZONE**

The street furniture zone is defined as
the section of the sidewalk between
the curb and the through zone in
which street furniture and amenities,
such as lighting, benches, newspaper
kiosks, utility poles, tree pits, and
bicycle parking are provided. The street
furniture zone may also consist of
green infrastructure elements, such as
rain gardens or flow-through planters.

**4 ENHANCEMENT/
BUFFER ZONE**

The enhancement/buffer zone is
the space immediately next to the
sidewalk that may consist of a variety
of different elements. These include
curb extensions, parklets, stormwater
management features, parking, bike
racks, bike share stations, and curbside
bike lanes or cycle tracks.

Sidewalk Design

The sidewalk is the area where people interface with one another and with businesses most directly in an urban environment. Designs that create a high-quality experience at street level will enhance the economic strength of commercial districts and the quality of life of neighborhoods.[2]

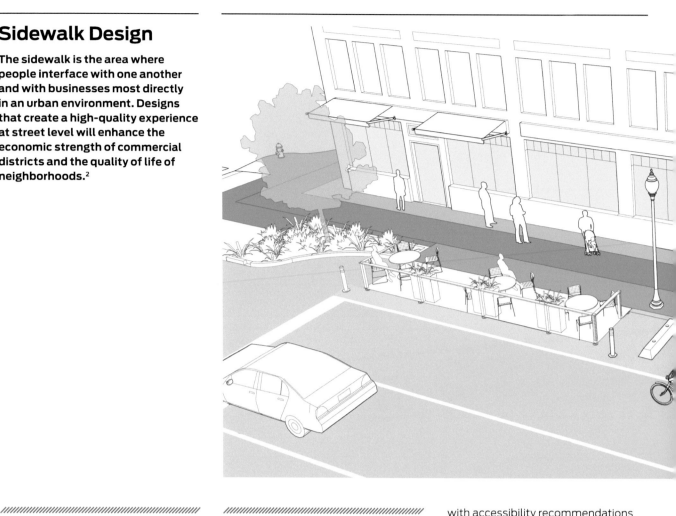

DISCUSSION

Sidewalks are an essential component of the urban environment and serve as key corridors for people, goods, and commerce. In accordance with ADA accessibility guidelines, sidewalks should be provided on all streets in urban areas.[3]

Numerous studies have shown that good pedestrian network connectivity and walkability have a positive impact on land values.[4]

Sidewalks have significant lifespans and can be maintained without replacement for 25 years or more, depending on the context.[5]

CRITICAL

Sidewalks have a desired minimum through zone of 6 feet and an absolute minimum of 5 feet. Where a sidewalk is directly adjacent to moving traffic, the desired minimum is 8 feet, providing a minimum 2-foot buffer for street furniture and utilities.[6]

Sidewalk design should go beyond the bare minimums in both width and amenities. Pedestrians and businesses thrive where sidewalks have been designed at an appropriate scale, with sufficient lighting, shade, and street-level activity. These considerations are especially important for streets with higher traffic speeds and volumes, where pedestrians may otherwise feel unsafe and avoid walking.

Sidewalks should be provided on both sides of all streets in all urban areas. On shared streets, the street itself serves as the path of travel and should be designed in accordance

with accessibility recommendations outlined in the shared street section of these guidelines. In certain instances, such as on more rural or suburban roads connecting urban areas, it may be advantageous to build a shared-use path adjacent to the main roadway as a substitute for a sidewalk. In this case, the shared use path should meet the general criteria to serve adequately as a sidewalk or pathway.

PHILADELPHIA, PA
The sidewalk on Walnut Street over the Schuylkill River was widened from 8 to 12 feet to provide a wider buffer with lighting.

Façades and storefronts should be designed to cater to the eye level of pedestrians. Strategies include:

- Lighting scaled to the pedestrian realm in addition to overhead lighting for vehicles.

- Benches and other seating platforms designed into the structure itself or placed within the frontage zone.

- Incentives to provide awnings, sidewalk cafes, and other elements that improve the comfort and appearance of the sidewalk.

- Where security concerns are present, use of permeable, rather than closed, metal shutters on storefronts at night *(above)*.

- Provision of adequate lighting beneath scaffolding and other construction sites.

The use of shoulders as a substitute for sidewalks is never justified in urban areas. Sidewalks should be delineated by a vertical and horizontal separation from moving traffic to provide an adequate buffer space and a sense of safety for pedestrians. Wide low-volume local or residential roads without sidewalks should be upgraded, but in the interim may be regulated as shared spaces or improved through the use of temporary materials where there is a potential danger to pedestrians.

Sidewalk design may be compromised by roadside design guidance that requires lateral offsets or clear zones forgiving to higher vehicle speeds. Use a lower design speed or widen the sidewalk to mitigate these impacts.

Delineation of a minimum setback from the curb is not a required feature in urban environments. For the purpose of maintenance, cities should evaluate the impact of street trees, signs, and other elements on the structural integrity of the curb and access needs for parked vehicles or loading/unloading.

Where transit stops are provided, bus shelters should be placed at the left or right edge of the walkway, but never directly within the path of travel. Where insufficient space exists, consider the application of a bus bulb.

Relocation of fixed objects, such as utility poles, light fixtures, and other street furniture should not impinge on or restrict the adjacent walkway. Walkways must be clear of fixed objects in coordination with ADA accessibility guidelines.[7]

Ensure that sidewalks are without major gaps or deformities that would make them non-traversable for wheelchairs and other mobility devices.

At driveways, sidewalks should be maintained at-grade through the conflict zone.

Any construction project that obstructs the sidewalk should be mitigated through the provision of a temporary sidewalk that affords a safe and convenient passage or clearly directs users to an equivalent nearby detour.

DOWNTOWN
Conventional Sidewalk

Sidewalks are central to pedestrian life. Cities can enhance the public realm by creating venues where people can observe street life and activity, especially in retail and commercial areas.

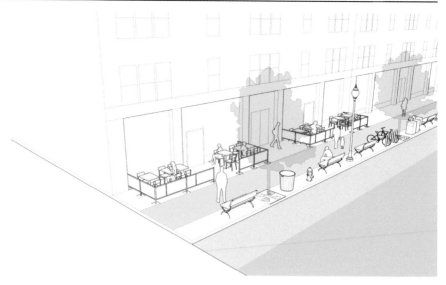

DOWNTOWN
Wide Sidewalk

From the 1960s through 1980s, many downtown sidewalks were widened as part of new downtown office tower developments. Wide downtown sidewalks benefit from public art, music, human-scale design features, and vendors to avoid feeling empty or oversized.

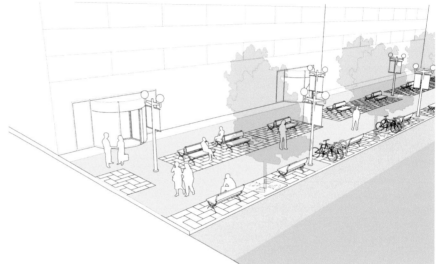

RECOMMENDED

Select street trees and tree wells whose roots have a limited impact on the integrity of the sidewalk's structure.

Sidewalk cafes foster street life and have the potential to increase business along a corridor. Where provided, sidewalk cafes should not impinge upon the accessible pedestrian pathway.

Where a city decides to repurpose a portion of the sidewalk as a raised bikeway, utilities and other street furniture should be relocated (in the facility's permanent reconstruction) to adequately separate pedestrian and bicycle traffic.

KANSAS CITY, MO
In retail districts, decorative materials and wide sidewalks support businesses.

NEIGHBORHOOD
Narrow Sidewalk

Narrow neighborhood sidewalks should be redesigned to provide a wider pedestrian through zone and street furniture zone whenever practicable.

RESIDENTIAL
Ribbon Sidewalk

Ribbon sidewalks are common in most residential areas. Design the pedestrian through zone to be roughly equal to the planted area, using pervious strips where applicable to help manage stormwater.

If a sidewalk is directly adjacent to the roadway, 2 feet should be added to the absolute minimum clear path width to ensure that there is sufficient space for roadside hardware and snow storage.[8] Parking provides a valuable buffer between the pedestrian and vehicle realm. Urban arterials or high-volume downtown streets directly abutting the pedestrian realm should be buffered in some capacity, whether through a street furniture zone, parking, cycle track, or other feature. Sidewalks of minimum dimensions directly adjacent to the traveled way should be avoided.

STREET TREES

Street trees enhance city streets both functionally and aesthetically. Trees provide shade to homes, businesses, and pedestrians. Street trees also have the potential to slow traffic speeds, especially when placed on a curb extension in line with on-street parking, and may increase pavement life by avoiding extreme heat. Aesthetically, street trees frame the street and the sidewalk as discrete public realms, enriching each with a sense of rhythm and human scale.

Requirements for tree spacing depend upon a number of key factors and should be tailored to the chosen species, standard (or desired) tree pit size, fixed

property lines, setback from curb, and integration with street lights and other furniture.

Street trees may be removed to satisfy sight distance or clear zone require-ments only in extreme cases, where the installation of traffic control devices has been precluded. Larger trees protect pedestrians from errant vehicles.

When pedestrian networks cross municipal boundaries, efforts should be made to ensure seamless continuity of the pedestrian infrastructure.

//

OPTIONAL

In newer residential areas, many streets have been constructed without sidewalks. If traffic volumes are sufficiently low in these areas, consider designating or upgrading these areas to shared streets. This requires the addition of specific traffic calming devices and regulations that offset potential conflicts with traffic accessing local properties.

Many older residential areas have trees whose roots have compromised the integrity of the sidewalk. On low-volume roads, consider the application of a curb extension that obviates the need to remove trees or the installation of a wider sidewalk during reconstruction.

Where pedestrian volumes create congested conditions along sidewalks, cities are encouraged to pursue temporary means to ease overflow from the sidewalk onto the streets. Interim elements, such as epoxied gravel pavements or temporary lane closures, may be able to provide an interim solution until a city can widen the walkway. If special events are anticipated to significantly increase pedestrian traffic, similar strategies should be pursued to ensure pedestrians are not forced into vehicular traffic.

Lane closures should be considered to ease sidewalk congestion during times with known high pedestrian volumes.

CLEAR ZONES

The concept of "clear zones" is sometimes cited in the highway design process. A clear zone represents an unobstructed, traversable area beyond the traveled way, often a paved or planted shoulder or a short setback on the sidewalk.[9] Clear zones provide a run-off zone for errant vehicles that have deviated from the main roadway and are intended to decrease the frequency and severity of fixed-object roadside crashes, forgiving driver error.[10]

While clear zones are applicable as a safety parameter for the Interstate and freeway system, in urban settings, destination of a minimum set back from the curb is not required. To the greatest extent possible, the lateral distance between the traveled way and the sidewalk (or parking lane) should be minimized, providing ample space for sidewalks and other amenities.[11]

Clear zones are applicable on rural highways with high vehicle speeds, not in urban areas.

Removal of roadside impediments (trees, street furniture, etc.) has an ambiguous safety record in urban environments and is at odds with city policies striving to increase pedestrian traffic and spur economic activity. Street trees and other roadside features are superior to wide shoulders or run-off zones, as they can decrease overall speeds and encourage a more pedestrian-friendly environment.

Curb Extensions

Curb extensions visually and physically narrow the roadway, creating safer and shorter crossings for pedestrians while increasing the available space for street furniture, benches, plantings, and street trees. They may be implemented on downtown, neighborhood, and residential streets, large and small. Curb extensions have multiple applications and may be segmented into various sub-categories, ranging from traffic calming to bus bulbs and midblock crossings.

APPLICATION

Curb extension is an umbrella term that encompasses several different treatments and applications. These include:

· Midblock curb extensions, known as pinchpoints or chokers, which may include cut-throughs for bicyclists.

· Curb extensions used as gateways to minor streets known as neckdowns.

· Offset curb extensions that force vehicles to move laterally, known as chicanes.

· Curb extensions at bus (or transit) stops, also known as bus bulbs.

· Conventional curb extensions, which are a recommended feature where there is on-street parking.

BENEFITS & CONSIDERATIONS

Curb extensions decrease the overall width of the roadway and can serve as a visual cue to drivers that they are entering a neighborhood street or area.

Curb extensions increase the overall visibility of pedestrians by aligning them with the parking lane and reducing the crossing distance for pedestrians, creating more time for preferential treatments, such as leading pedestrian interval and transit signal priority.[1]

Curb extensions tighten intersection curb radii and encourage slower turning speeds.

Installation of curb extensions may require moving a fire hydrant to maintain adequate curbside access in case of a fire. In such cases, a curb extension may incur additional expense or be reoriented to avoid conflict with the hydrant.[2]

Used as a bus bulb, curb extensions may improve bus travel times by reducing the amount of time a bus takes to merge with traffic after boarding. Bus bulbs also help to prevent motorists from double parking in the bus stop.[3]

Where application of a curb extension adversely impacts drainage, curb extensions may be designed as edge islands with a 1–2-foot gap from the curb or a trench drain.

Curb extensions can be implemented using low-cost, interim materials. In such cases, curb extensions should be demarcated from the existing road-bed using temporary curbs, bollards, planters, or striping.

Gateway

Curb extensions are often applied at the mouth of an intersection. When installed at the entrance to a residential or low-speed street, a curb extension is referred to as a "gateway" treatment and is intended to mark the transition to a slower speed street.

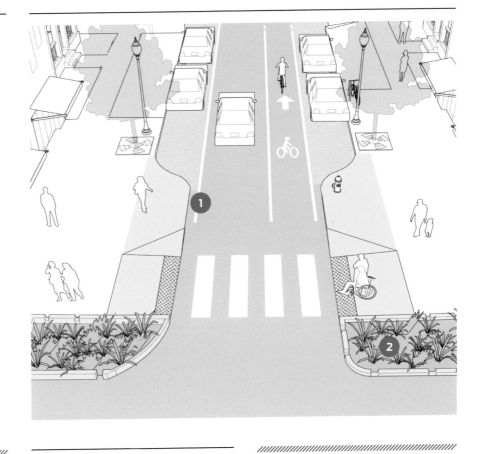

CRITICAL

The length of a curb extension should at least be equal to the width of the crosswalk, but is recommended to extend to the advanced stop bar.

RECOMMENDED

1 A curb extension should generally be 1–2 feet narrower than the parking lane, except where the parking lane is treated with materials that integrate it into the structure of the sidewalk.

NEW YORK, NY

Curb extensions should be installed whenever on-street parking is present to increase visibility, reduce the crossing distance, provide extra queuing space, and allow for enhancements, such as seating or greenery.

2 Combine stormwater management features, such as bioswales or rain gardens, with curb extensions to absorb rainwater and reduce the impervious surface area of a street.

INDIANAPOLIS, IN
Curb extensions may be combined with bioswales in order to decrease puddling at crosswalks.

OPTIONAL

Curb extensions may be treated with corner street furniture and other amenities that enhance the public realm.

NEW YORK, NY

In advance of a full reconstruction, gateways can be designed using striping or signage that communicates the entrance into a slow zone.

Pinchpoint

Curb extensions may be applied at midblock to slow traffic speeds and add public space. When utilized as a traffic calming treatment, mid-block curb extensions are referred to as "pinchpoints" or "chokers".

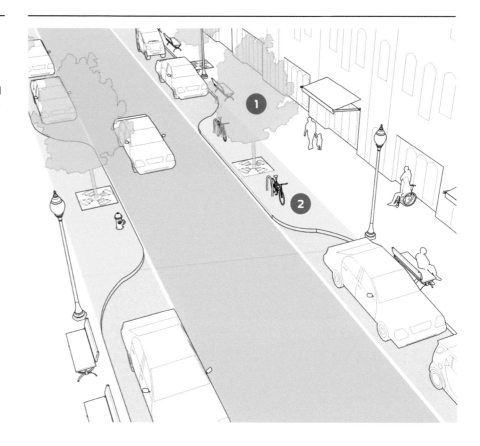

RECOMMENDED

1 Plant street trees on curb extensions aligned to the parking lane to narrow the overall profile of the roadway. Before installing street trees on the curb extension, assess surrounding utilities to ensure that the trees' roots will not damage under-ground infrastructure.

OPTIONAL

Pinchpoints can facilitate midblock pedestrian crossings of low-volume streets. These crossings do not need to be marked, unless volumes exceed 2,000–3,000 vehicles per day or midblock destinations warrant an enhanced treatment.

2 Bicycle racks can be combined with curb extensions, especially in areas where bicycle parking is insufficient or demand for long-term or short-term parking is unmet.

NEW YORK, NY
6 1/2 Avenue in New York City connects a series of privately-owned public spaces that cut midblock through Midtown. The visibility of crossing pedestrians was improved here using pinchpoints constructed with interim materials.

Chicane

Offset curb extensions on residential or low volume downtown streets create a chicane effect that slows traffic speeds considerably. Chicanes increase the amount of public space available on a corridor and can be activated using benches, bicycle parking, and other amenities.

RECOMMENDED

A chicane design may warrant additional signing and striping to ensure that drivers are aware of a slight bend in the roadway.

OPTIONAL

Where application of a curb extension adversely impacts drainage, curb extensions may be designed as edge islands with a 1–2-foot gap from the curb.

Curb extensions can be implemented using low-cost or temporary materials. In such cases, curb extensions should be demarcated from the existing roadbed using temporary curbs, bollards, planters, or striping.

SAN FRANCISCO, CA
A chicane was added to slow speeds entering this residential block.

Chicanes may be designed using a return angle of 45 degrees, or a more gradual taper and transition, resulting in an S-shaped roadway.

A chicane configuration may also be created using a "checkered" parking scheme.

Bus Bulbs

Bus bulbs are curb extensions that align the bus stop with the parking lane, allowing buses to stop and board passengers without ever leaving the travel lane. Bus bulbs help buses move faster and more reliably by decreasing the amount of time lost when merging in and out of traffic.

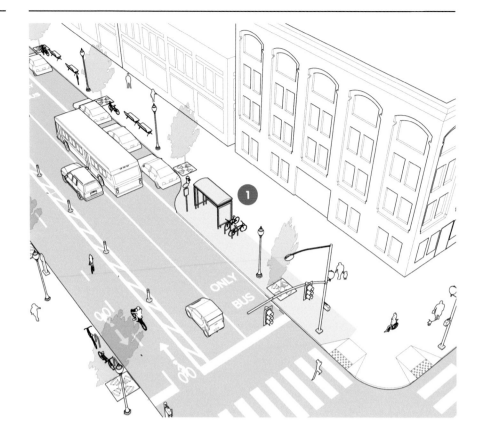

CRITICAL

Bus bulbs have a desired length of the equivalent of two buses for a route with frequent service (e.g., 140 feet for two articulated buses). Routes with less frequent service may have the length of one bus from the front of the vehicle to the back door (e.g., 30 feet). The width should reflect the need for maneuvering and accommodation of bus shelters, at least 6 feet but preferably 8–10 feet.[4]

Cities should work with transit providers to determine the clear width necessary to deploy a wheelchair-accessible lift onto the bus bulb.

A bus bulb should be roughly equal to the width of the parking lane with a return angle of 45 degrees.[5]

SEATTLE, WA
The bike lane can be routed behind a bus boarding island.

RECOMMENDED

Use cut-throughs for curbside bike lanes and cycle tracks at intersections and midblock bus bulbs. Curbside bike lanes should not be dropped on the approach to an intersection with a curb extension.

Where a near-side bus bulb is combined with a turn restriction, design the curb to self-enforce the turn restriction and monitor closely to ensure that transit vehicles are not suffering from delays.

1 Bus bulbs should be equipped with transit shelters whenever possible. Shelters make transit more attractive and may be combined with off-board fare collection for faster payment options.

OPTIONAL

When applied near-side, bus bulbs may require right-turn-on-red restrictions where motorists are likely to queue in the right-hand lane. At these locations, enforcement is absolutely necessary to ensure that the curb extension serves its purpose successfully.

Bus bulbs may be combined with amenities such as wayfinding maps, plantings, and trees to enhance the overall transit user experience.

Vertical Speed Control Elements

Vertical speed control elements manage traffic speeds and reinforce safe, pedestrian-friendly speeds. These devices may be appropriate on a range of street types, but are most widely applied along neighborhood, residential, or low-speed streets where freight traffic is discouraged. They may be installed in tandem with horizontal traffic calming measures such as curb extensions or chicanes, or applied individually on streets with a constrained right-of-way.

APPLICATION

Vertical speed control elements should be applied where the target speed of the roadway cannot be achieved through the use of conventional traffic calming elements, such as medians, narrower roadways or lanes, curb extensions, enforcement, or lower speed limits.

Streets with speed limits of 30 mph and under are good candidates for vertical speed control, especially where those streets have higher than desired operating speeds or are used by cut-through traffic on a regular basis.

BENEFITS & CONSIDERATIONS

Vertical speed control has been shown to slow traffic speeds, creating a safer and more attractive environment.[1]

Vertical speed control elements are most effectively implemented at a neighborhood level, rather than by request on a single street. Designate "Slow Zones" where traffic calming treatments should be targeted or coordinated in a comprehensive way.[2]

In colder climates, vertical traffic calming must be designed to permit snow removal. Cities must work cooperatively with local agencies responsible for street sweeping and snow removal to ensure that they do not significantly hinder operations or damage speed control elements.

Vertical speed control elements may deter cut-through traffic but exacerbate traffic conditions on surrounding streets as a result. Monitor the impact of traffic calming treatments at the network level or install on a pilot basis to assess potential impacts.

Unless otherwise desired, vertical traffic calming should reduce a street's target speed to 20 mph or less.

Implementation may be carried out on a trial basis to gauge residents' support prior to finalizing the design. Temporary speed humps, tables, and cushions should be used with caution as they can diminish residents' opinions due to unappealing design and reduced functionality.

The ideal spacing for vertical speed controls depends on the specific profile of the street as well as horizontal or regulatory traffic calming measures. Spacing should be consistent and determined according to the desired target speed and operating speed of the road as well as volume, context, and the overall number of driveways. Where drivers accelerate to unsafe speeds between speed controls, spacing may need to be reevaluated.

Speed Hump

Speed humps are parabolic vertical traffic calming devices intended to slow traffic speeds on low-volume, low-speed roads. Speed humps are 3–4 inches high and 12–14 feet wide, with a ramp length of 3–6 feet, depending on target speed. Speed humps reduce speeds to 15–20 mph and are often referred to as "bumps" on signage and by the general public.

CRITICAL

Speed humps shall not be placed in front of driveways or other significant access areas. Where frequent driveways make the application of a speed hump difficult, reduce the overall size of the speed hump, or work with local residents to find a workable solution.

RECOMMENDED

Vertical speed control elements should be accompanied by a sign warning drivers of the upcoming device. (MUTCD W17-1).

Speed humps should be designed to the following criteria:

- Slopes should not exceed 1:10 or be less steep than 1:25.

- Side slopes on tapers should be no greater than 1:6.

- The vertical lip should be no more than a quarter-inch high.

Locate vertical speed control elements where there is sufficient visibility and available lighting.

Spacing for vertical speed controls should be determined based on the target speed of the roadway. Speed humps should be spaced no more than a maximum of 500 feet apart to achieve an 85th percentile speed of 25–35 mph. To achieve greater speed reductions, space speed humps close together.

NORWALK, CT

Many residential streets have ample right-of-way for two lanes of travel plus parking, resulting in higher than desired speeds.

WASHINGTON, D.C.

Speed humps are almost exclusively used in residential areas and are often paired with signs (MUTCD W17-1).

Speed humps may be applied on 1-way or 2-way roads.

Speed Table

Speed tables are midblock traffic calming devices that raise the entire wheelbase of a vehicle to reduce its traffic speed. Speed tables are longer than speed humps and flat-topped, with a height of 3–3.5 inches and a length of 22 feet. Vehicle operating speeds for streets with speed tables range from 25–45 mph, depending on the spacing.[3] Speed tables may be used on collector streets and/or transit and emergency response routes. Where applied, speed tables may be designed as raised midblock crossings, often in conjunction with curb extensions.

RECOMMENDED

Speed tables should be accompanied by a sign warning drivers (MUTCD W17-1).

Speed tables should be designed to the following criteria:

- Slopes should not exceed 1:10 or be less steep than 1:25.
- Side slopes on tapers should be no greater than 1:6.
- The vertical lip should be no more than a quarter-inch high.

Speed tables should not be applied on streets wider than 50 feet. On 2-way streets, speed tables may be applied in both directions.

Where a speed table coincides with a crossing or crosswalk, it should be designed as a raised crosswalk.

Locate vertical speed control elements where there is sufficient visibility and available lighting.

OPTIONAL

Speed tables are often designed using unit pavers or other distinctive materials. Distinctive materials may require additional maintenance responsibilities but help to highlight and define the speed table for both bicyclists and pedestrians.

SOMERVILLE, MA
This speed table has been designed as a raised crossing.

Speed Cushion

Speed cushions are either speed humps or speed tables that include wheel cutouts to allow large vehicles to pass unaffected, while reducing passenger car speeds. They can be offset to allow unimpeded passage by emergency vehicles and are typically used on key emergency response routes. Speed cushions extend across one direction of travel from the centerline, with longitudinal gap provided to allow wide wheelbase vehicles to avoid going over the hump.

CRITICAL

When vertical speed control is implemented on major emergency access routes, use speed cushions designed to accommodate the wheelbase of the emergency vehicle.[4]

RECOMMENDED

Vertical speed control should be accompanied by a sign warning drivers (MUTCD W17-1).

Vertical speed control elements should be designed to the following criteria:

- Slopes should not exceed 1:10 or be less steep than 1:25.

- Side slopes on tapers should be no greater than 1:6.

- The vertical lip should be no more than a quarter-inch high.

Locate speed cushions where there is sufficient visibility and available lighting.

OPTIONAL

Bus routes may have speed cushions installed on certain routes. Work with local transit providers and bus companies to ensure that drivers are aware of traffic calming devices and can effectively use wheel cut-outs provided.

Speed cushions allow emergency vehicles to pass their wheels on either side of the raised area.

EMERGENCY VEHICLES

Emergency services should act in coordination with transportation departments, recognizing that reducing speeds and volumes on local roadways benefits overall safety goals by reducing crash frequency and severity. Develop an emergency response route classification map at the onset of the planning process. Emergency vehicle response times should be considered where vertical speed control mechanisms are used. Because emergency vehicles have a wider wheel base than passenger cars, speed cushions allow them to pass unimpeded while slowing most traffic.

Strategies include the following:

· Seek approval by emergency response officials for treatments on emergency response routes.

· Allow a limited set of emergency vehicle-friendly traffic calming techniques on emergency response routes.

· Estimate travel time impacts on emergency vehicle response time and define goals to evaluate during a trial.

· Implement speed management treatments on a trial basis and work with emergency response officials to determine whether permanent features are appropriate.

Transit Streets

Building streets to support transit entails considering every passenger's trip from start to finish. People walking to the transit stop should find their path safe and inviting. Dedicated transit lanes, appropriate base signal timings, and operational traffic improvements ensure that the transit vehicle experiences minimal wait time at intersections and can move freely regardless of traffic congestion, providing a passenger experience competitive with driving. Transit stops also play an important role as part of the streetscape. They have the potential to enhance the quality of the public realm when integrated with certain key features, such as quality bus shelters, wayfinding maps, and real-time information systems.

The recommendations here focus on bus transit. However, many of the same set of treatments would also apply to streetcar or on-street light rail transit.

Dedicated Curbside/ Offset Bus Lanes

APPLICATION

Dedicated bus lanes are typically applied on major routes with frequent headways (10 minutes at peak) or where traffic congestion may significantly affect reliability. As on-time performance degrades, consider more aggressive treatments to speed transit service. Agencies may set ridership or service standard benchmarks for transitioning bus service to a transit-only facility.[1] Lanes may be located immediately at the curb or in an offset configuration, replacing the rightmost travel lane on a street where parking is permitted.

PORTLAND, OR
Curbside bus stops paired with parking restrictions make accessing the stop easier for the operator.

NEW YORK, NY
In an offset bus lane design, drivers can park to the right of the bus lane and passengers board at bus bulbs.

BENEFITS & CONSIDERATIONS

Bus lanes reduce delays due to traffic congestion and help raise the visibility of the high-quality service.

Curbside and offset bus lanes are subject to encroachment due to double-parking, deliveries, or taxicabs. Strict enforcement is necessary to maintain their use and integrity.[2]

CRITICAL

1 BUS-ONLY pavement markings should be applied to emphasize the lane and to deter drivers from using it (MUTCD 3D-01).

NEW YORK, NY
Red paint, BUS ONLY markings, and white striping separate the transit lane from travel lanes.

2 Dedicated lanes should be separated from other traffic using solid single or double white stripes. A solid single white line conveys that crossing into the bus lane is discouraged, whereas a double solid white line means that encroachment is legally prohibited. (MUTCD 3B-04)

RECOMMENDED

Bus lane width should be determined based on the available street space and the competing needs of bicyclists, pedestrians, and motorists. The minimum width of a curbside bus lane is 11 feet. The minimum width of an offset bus lane is 10 feet.

GLENDALE, CA
Bus bulbs provide space for transit passenger amenities while maintaining through space for pedestrians behind the shelter.

3 Bus bulbs should be installed if lanes are offset. Bus lanes may have complementary effects with other bus rapid transit elements, such as off-board fare payment and transit signal priority.

Transit signal priority should be implemented wherever feasible to reduce transit delays due to traffic signals. Shorter signal cycles also process movements more efficiently and maximize the usefulness of the transit signal priority system.

Red colored paint should be applied to emphasize the lane and to deter drivers from using it. Red paint has higher installation and maintenance costs, but has been shown to deter both unauthorized driving and parking in the bus lane.[3]

Prohibiting right turns during hours when the dedicated lane is in effect or otherwise separating these movements helps to keep the lane clear.

OPTIONAL

Bus lanes may be separated with soft barriers (i.e., rumble strips) or hard barriers (concrete curbs). If hard separation is used, bus lanes should be designed to allow passing at selected points.

Dedicated bus lanes may be implemented on a 24-hour basis or managed for specific intervals of the day only.

ALEXANDRIA, VA

Dedicated Curbside Bus Lane

Dedicated Offset Bus Lane

Dedicated Median Bus Lanes

APPLICATION

Dedicated median bus lanes are typically applied on major routes with frequent headways or where traffic congestion may significantly affect reliability. Median bus lanes are applied along the centerline of a multilane roadway and should be paired with accessible transit stops in the roadway median where needed.

BENEFITS & CONSIDERATIONS

Dedicated median bus lanes eliminate conflicts with potential drop-offs, deliveries, or illegal parking along the roadway edge.

Intersections require turning provisions for vehicles to avoid conflicts with the through movements of the transit vehicles. Enforcement is necessary to ensure their effectiveness.

PHOENIX, AZ
Turn signals ensure that vehicles do not block transit ways.

Installation should be coordinated with land use changes that maximize economic growth potential. Setback guidelines and other land use regulations should be tailored to create a more inviting pedestrian realm.

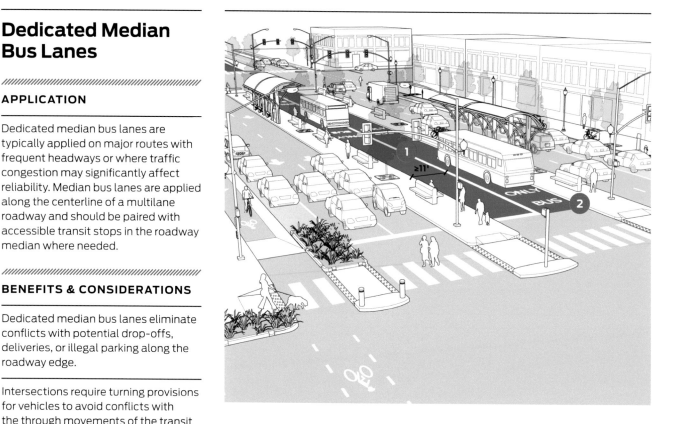

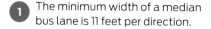

CRITICAL

1. The minimum width of a median bus lane is 11 feet per direction.

2. Dedicated bus transit lanes require median boarding islands in the roadway at each stop. These stops must be fully accessible and lead to safe, controlled crosswalks or other crossings.[4]

For dedicated median bus lanes, BUS ONLY pavement markings (MUTCD 3D-01) emphasize the lane and deter drivers from using it.

Dedicated lanes should be separated from other traffic with solid single or double white stripes, at a minimum.

RECOMMENDED

Red colored paint should be applied to emphasize dedicated median bus lanes and deter drivers from using them.

Separation of the dedicated median bus lane with soft barriers (i.e., rumble strips) and/or hard barriers (concrete curbs) should be considered to reduce encroachment from moving vehicles.

OPTIONAL

Dedicated median bus lanes should have complementary rapid transit elements, such as off-board fare payment and transit signal priority.

Contra-Flow Bus Lanes

APPLICATION

Contra-flow bus lanes are typically applied to bus routes to create strategic, efficient connections rather than as a continuous application along a corridor.

The ideal contra-flow bus lane is designed similar to a regular 2-way street, with non-transit vehicles barred from using the lane or lanes in one direction.

BENEFITS & CONSIDERATIONS

Contra-flow bus lanes may enable connectivity and shorten travel times for bus routes.

When there is illegal encroachment by non-transit uses, contra-flow bus lanes will be ineffective.

CRITICAL

At contra-flow bus lanes, ONE-WAY, DO NOT ENTER and turn prohibition signs should be supplemented with an EXCEPT BUSES and BICYCLES plaque.

A double-yellow centerline marking (MUTCD 3D-02) or buffer marking (MUTCD 3D-02) should be applied to separate contra-flow bus traffic from opposing traffic. If used, the buffer should be a minimum of 3 feet wide.

BUS ONLY markings (MUTCD 3D-01) should be applied to emphasize the lane and to deter drivers from using it.

Strict enforcement is necessary to maintain the lane's use and integrity.

Traffic signal coordination should be updated to reflect the 2-way flow of buses.

Arrow pavement markings (MUTCD 3B-20) should be used to indicate the path of travel.

RECOMMENDED

A 2-lane-wide profile of 22–24 feet is preferred for contra-flow bus travel. This allows buses to pass other buses (and stopped vehicles) and makes the street design clearer to pedestrians. Depending on the length of the contra-flow lane and the available roadway width, a narrower lane may be acceptable.

MINNEAPOLIS, MN
This double bus lane allows vehicles to pass each other.

Red colored paint should be applied to emphasize the lane and deter drivers from using it.

OPTIONAL

Bicycle traffic may be encouraged to use the contra-flow bus lane in certain instances, as long as the lane is wide enough to allow safe passing. Where bicycle traffic is permitted, a ONE WAY-EXCEPT BUSES, BIKES (MUTCD 9B-01) sign should be used.

Curbs, medians, or bollards may be applied to deter encroaching vehicles, though access to the curb should be maintained for emergency vehicles.

Bus Stops

Bus stop planning and design involves thinking about existing and new stops from both the macro framework of system design and the micro level of conditions around the transit stop. Many cities and transit agencies have developed internal guidelines to determine the appropriate spacing and design criteria for particular transit routes and stops.

DISCUSSION

Surface bus routes, especially those without dedicated lanes, should have clearly marked bus stops that call attention to the stop and explain the route. Frequency and placement of the bus stops should serve the maximum number of destinations while minimizing delays.

SAN FRANCISCO, CA
A midblock bus stop with a bus bulb.

There are generally three categories of bus stop locations:

1. **Far-side bus stops** are the most common and are generally preferred by designers. They allow pedestrians to cross behind the bus, which is safer than crossing in front of the bus. On multilane roadways, they also increase the visibility of crossing pedestrians for drivers waiting at the signal.

BOSTON, MA

2. **Near-side bus stops** should ideally be used in these circumstances:

   · On long blocks where the near-side stop interfaces better with pedestrian destinations, such as parks, subway entrances, waterfronts, and schools.

   · Where the bus route is on a 1-way street with one lane of traffic and does not permit passing.

   · Where specific traffic calming features or parking provisions restrict the use of far-side stops.

   · Where access to a senior center or hospital is located at the near-side of the intersection.

   · Where driveways or alleys make the far-side stop location problematic.

SAN FRANCISCO, CA

3. **Midblock bus stops** require more space between parked cars and other barriers to allow buses to enter and exit the stop, except where there is a bus bulb. They are recommended for:

   · Long blocks with important destinations midblock, such as waterfronts, campuses, and parks.

   · Major transit stops with multiple buses queuing.

Far-side Bus Stop

CRITICAL

1 Bus stops must have safe access via sidewalks and appropriate street crossing locations. Where possible, pedestrian crossings should be accommodated behind the departing transit vehicle.

The amount of sidewalk space around a bus stop should meet the intended demand and ridership levels. Streets with insufficient queuing space at bus stops should consider the implementation of a bus bulb or dedicated waiting area.

Bus stops are required to meet ADA standards, including the provision of landing pads and curb heights that allow for buses to load passengers in wheelchairs.

RECOMMENDED

2 Bus shelters should be provided for stops on routes with high boarding numbers.[5]

3 Bus bulbs should be applied where offset bus lanes are provided, where merging into traffic is difficult, or where passengers need a dedicated waiting area. Where applied, bus bulbs should be 40 feet long and at least 6-feet wide with no step to the sidewalk (based on a 40-foot bus). If there is a step to the sidewalk, the bus bulb should be at least 10 feet in width or be designed to accommodate the length of the wheelchair ramp used on most standard 40-foot buses.

If parking is not allowed on the street, a bus layby (also known as a bus bay) may be built into the sidewalk so that the bus pulls out of traffic. This should only be considered in locations with wide enough sidewalks, and where the bus will not be delayed substantially by pulling back into traffic.

4 Information provided to riders at a bus or transit stop should include an agency logo or visual marker, station name, route map, and schedule. Bus stops should include a system and/or route map and schedule on the bus shelter or other street furniture.

Adequate lighting should be installed around bus stops and shelters to ensure personal safety and security.

BOSTON, MA
This stop contains basic information about the schedule, route, and map.

The vast majority of bus stops are located at intersections. In many states, access management guidelines ban driveways within 100–300 feet of an intersection, depending on whether the intersection is signalized or unsignalized, as well as the roadway's speed limit. If access management guidelines are enforced actively and retroactively, passengers can be spared waiting in driveways for the bus.[6]

OPTIONAL

Real-time information systems may be added at bus stops to enhance the rider experience and create a predictable travel experience for riders.

At major bus stops, cities may enhance the experience of passengers and passersby through the addition of shelters, benches, area maps, plantings, vendors, or artworks.

PORTLAND, OR
This stop serves several bus routes. The shelter blocks rain but maintains visibility. Real-time information gives the arrival time of the next buses.

Stormwater Management

Sustainable stormwater management treats and slows runoff from impervious roadways, sidewalks, and building surfaces. In urban areas, natural drainage patterns have changed over time due to the incremental increase of impervious surface areas. Hardscapes, such as concrete and asphalt, prevent rainfall from being absorbed at the source. Increased stormwater flows and pollutants enter the subgrade pipe network as a result, burdening the municipal wastewater system (in the case of a Combined Sewer System) or discharging into surface water bodies. High-velocity discharge risks the erosion or flooding of local streams and creeks, destroying natural habitats.[1]

APPLICATION

Conventional stormwater management infrastructure has been engineered to move the largest volume of water from a site as quickly as possible, collecting surface runoff in subsurface structures.[2] Sustainable stormwater management captures water closer to the source, reducing combined sewer overflows (CSOs), ponding, and roadway flooding. In the process, rain water issues as an asset to improve urban ecology, microclimates, air quality, and the aesthetic quality of the public realm.

Sustainable stormwater management aims to achieve the following goals:

Improve water quality

Vegetated strips and swales filter and reduce sediment and filter pollutants through settling, physical filtration in the soil matrix, biological breakdown by microbes, and nutrient uptake by plants.

Detain stormwater flows

Stormwater runoff is detained in facilities, such as flow-through planters, pervious pavements, and bioswales. Detaining the flows mitigates the peak flow rates from the rain event, which in turn helps reduce erosion, loss of nutrients, scouring, and load-carrying capacity.[3]

Reduce stormwater volumes

Overall stormwater runoff volumes may be reduced by designing facilities that absorb and infiltrate rain water in place. Water-tolerant plant root systems maintain the porosity of the soil while taking up excess water in the stormwater facility.

Relieve burden on municipal waste systems

Sustainable stormwater systems reduce the amount of stress on a city's wastewater treatment facilities, and may reduce long-term costs if applied at a citywide scale.[4] Unlike traditional infrastructure, which does not add any additional value beyond its stormwater conveyance function, green infrastructure can be incorporated into neighborhood parks and landscaping.

BENEFITS & CONSIDERATIONS

Sustainable stormwater management can prove less costly than upgrading large sub-grade pipe networks, and allows for flexible, modular installation.[5]

Maintenance agreements are necessary to establish responsibility for the upkeep of the facility. Agreements may be secured through a specific city agency, neighborhood or business association, or be assumed by the adjacent business or property owner.[6]

Facility design must account for the physical constraints of the site, the presence of subsurface utilities, the local climate, and the feasibility of maintenance agreements. An experienced geotechnical engineer should verify partial or full infiltration conditions of the native soils. Native soil conditions, site slopes, native plantings, and location within the existing watershed should all be considered in the design process. Infiltration facilities should only be located in Class A or B soils.[7]

Bioswales

Bioswales are vegetated, shallow, landscaped depressions designed to capture, treat, and infiltrate stormwater runoff as it moves downstream. They are typically sized to treat the water quality event, also known as the "first flush," which is the first and often most polluted volume of water resulting from a storm event. Bioswales are the most effective type of green infrastructure facility in slowing runoff velocity and cleansing water while recharging the underlying groundwater table. They have flexible siting requirements, allowing them to be integrated with medians, cul-de-sacs, bulb outs, and other public space or traffic calming strategies.

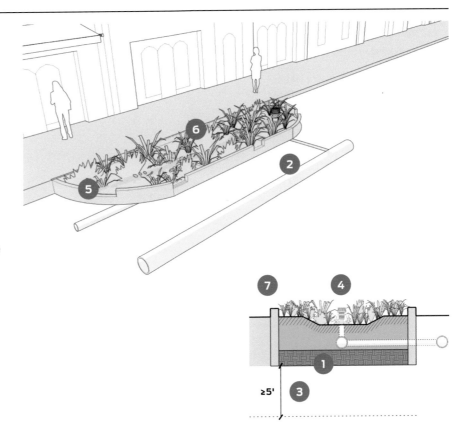

CRITICAL

1 Bioswales require appropriate media composition for soil construction. The engineered soil mixture should consist of 5% maximum clay content.

Ensure that infiltration rates meet their minimum and maximum criteria. The engineered soil mixture must be designed to pass 5–10 inches of rain water per hour.

Verify that underlying native soils are not contaminated prior to implementation. Prior contamination may undermine the purpose of the facility and must be remediated before installation. Infiltration facilities should only be located in class A or B soils.

Bioswales have a slight longitudinal slope that moves water along the surface to allow sediments and pollutants to settle out. In-place infiltration then allows localized groundwater recharge. Ideal side slopes are 4:1, with a maximum slope of 3:1.

2 Protect adjacent subsurface infrastructure by maintaining minimum clearances. Install waterproof liners as separation barriers or construct a deep curb to separate the roadbed subgrade or parallel utility line from the facility.

3 Maintain a 5-foot minimum clearance from the bottom of the bioswale to high groundwater table.

4 Raise the overflow/bypass drain system approximately 6 inches above the soil surface to manage storms larger than the water quality event.

5 Runoff that enters the bioswale in a sheetflow fashion requires that the edge of the bioswale be flush with grade. Where curbs are necessary, intermittently space curb cuts to allow runoff to enter and be treated within the swale. Both sheetflow and curb cut systems must allow for a minimum 2-inch drop in grade between the street grade and the finished grade of the facility. Curb cuts should be at least 18 inches wide. Depending on the site grading, curb cuts may be spaced from 3–15 feet apart.

RECOMMENDED

6 Bioswales should be composed of diverse, native vegetation. Vegetation selection should consider species compatibility, minimum irrigation requirements, and the potential for wildlife habitat creation.

To reduce exit velocities and prevent erosion, use pretreatment exit energy dissipaters, such as rocks.

If the longitudinal slope exceeds 4%, utilize check dams, berms or weirs to create a step-down gradient. Limit the maximum ponding depth to 6–12 inches.

7 Discourage pedestrian trampling by using low curbs or barriers, or hardy vegetative ground covers.

Bioswales are not recommended in locations with low infiltration rates because standing water, localized flooding, and other issues can cause problems within the street and sidewalk in an urban environment.

Flow-Through Planters

Flow-through planters are hard-edged stormwater management facilities with an impermeable base. Appropriate for infiltration-preclusive or high-density urban areas, flow-through planters treat water by allowing runoff to soak through its soil matrix and filter into an underdrain system.

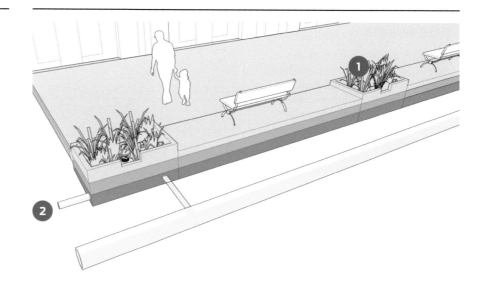

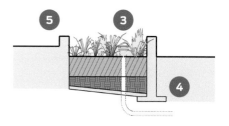

CRITICAL

1 Locate flow-through planters on non-infiltration areas, constrained sites next to buildings, areas with setback limitations, poorly draining soils, steep slopes (>4%), or areas with contaminated soils.

Use appropriate media composition for soil construction. The engineered soil mixture should consist of 5% maximum clay content.

2 Install a perforated pipe at the base of the facility to collect the treated runoff.

3 Use a raised drain to divert stormwater that exceeds the water quality event directly into drain system.

Install a downspout inlet or other conveyance sized for the water quality event and located to maximize treatment within the planter.

Provide a maximum 6-inch ponding depth for typical plant palettes. Deeper ponding depths require specialized planting palettes and should be avoided.

The drain rock layer must be clean and wrapped in filter fabric to protect the void space in the drain rock layer.

The planter must be designed to drain within 24 hours.

RECOMMENDED

Use native plantings that can handle seasonal flooding and require minimal irrigation.

OPTIONAL

4 Structured footing may be needed given sidewalk or street conditions to prevent lateral movement of the walls of the flow-through planter.

5 Discourage pedestrian trampling and reduce soil compaction by using low barriers or hardy vegetative ground covers. Barriers may be designed into the planter structure as streetside seating.

Pervious Strips

Pervious strips are long, linear landscaped areas or linear areas of pervious pavement that capture and slow runoff. Depending on the underlying subsurface soil conditions, pervious strips can provide some infiltration, but to a much lesser extent than bioswales. Pervious strips offer an inexpensive initial step in urban stormwater management but are unlikely to provide enough capacity for treatment of a street's full water quality event.

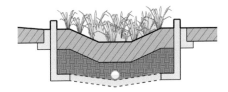

CRITICAL

1 Integrate pervious strips with sidewalks, medians, curbs, and other features. Depending on the desired configuration, pervious strips may treat either sheet flow or more channelized flow. Pervious strips require long, continuous spaces to treat and filter pollutants.

2 As required, install a perforated pipe at the base of the facility to collect the treated runoff.

Use a maximum 2% gentle side slope to direct flow into the facility.

Protect adjacent subsurface infrastructure by maintaining a minimum clearance, installing waterproof liners as separation barriers, or by constructing a deep curb to separate the roadbed subgrade or parallel utility line from the facility.

RECOMMENDED

Where possible, cluster public furniture and utility appurtenances to maximize the contiguous linear space for pervious strips and minimize conflicts.

Design the volume and flow capacity based on the contributing watershed area and design storm runoff.

Infiltrate if underlying soil is of an appropriate type for infiltration and there are no conflicts with underlying utilities.

3 Reduce irrigation requirements of pervious strips by utilizing pervious pavements and native plants. Native landscaped areas are generally preferable because they will generate less runoff and can help mitigate the urban heat island effect. Native plants increase biodiversity, act as a pollinator habitat, and are well-adapted to the regional climate, increasing their chances for survival.

Use a "green gutter" design with a flat bottom and vertical containment system.[8] This includes a very shallow (maximum 4-inch stormwater runoff detention) and thin (maximum 3-feet cross dimension) linear facility.

OPTIONAL

For additional runoff control on slopes exceeding 4%, consider the use of adjustable weirs, berms, check dams, or modified catchbasins that feed into the bioswale or permeable system.

Long, linear spaces may be integrated with urban agriculture programs.

Pervious Pavement

Pervious pavement effectively treats, detains, and infiltrates stormwater runoff where landscape-based strategies are restricted or less desired. Pervious pavements have multiple applications, including sidewalks, street furniture zones, and entire roadways (or just their parking lane or gutter strip portions). Treatments should be tailored to their specific climate and available maintenance capacities.

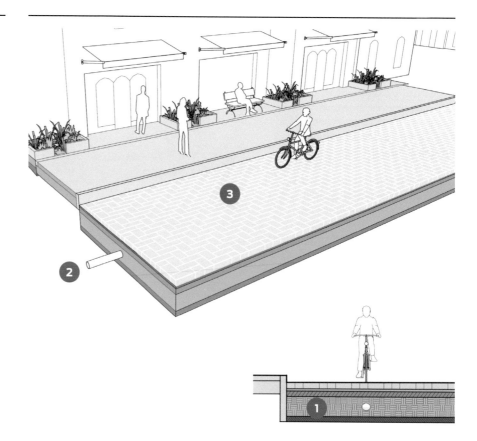

CRITICAL

Pervious pavements must be designed to account for the native subsoil infiltration rate. The depth of the pervious layer, void space, and the infiltration rate of the underlying soils result in the desired storage volume and intended drain time of the facility.

1 Prior to installation, verify that underlying native soils are not contaminated. A full geotechnical evaluation is required to determine the permeability, height of the water table, and depth to bedrock. Many urban areas have significant swaths of unclassified urban fill that may cause issues if not remediated.

Based on the potential vehicle usage and loading, verify the structural stability of the sub-grade materials. For example, some decorative pavers may be more susceptible to shifting than others, and are thus more appropriate for use in pedestrian- and bike-only areas.

In cold climates, use biodegradable, non-corrosive de-icing agents, such as BX36, GEN3, and BetaFrost.

The drain rock layer must be clean and wrapped in filter fabric.

Protect the adjacent subsurface infrastructure by maintaining minimum clearances, installing waterproof liners as separation barriers, or constructing a deep curb to separate the roadbed subgrade or parallel utility line from the facility.

In cold climates, salt should be applied in moderation to reduce contamination of the subsoil. Plowing should be done carefully, and abrasives, such as sand or cinders, should be avoided to preserve the integrity of the pavement system.

RECOMMENDED

2 Utilize an underdrain system to treat overflow, or if partial infiltration is preferred, to convey remaining runoff to the municipal sewer system.

Pervious pavement should drain within 48 hours.

Pervious pavements often require ongoing cleaning (vacuuming or power washing) to remove silt from the void spaces to maintain infiltration performance.

OPTIONAL

3 Selection of pavements, such as permeable pavers, permeable concrete, permeable asphalt, or other materials, should be based on engineering constraints and the surrounding street context.[9]

Interim Design Strategies

With limited funding streams, complex approval and regulatory processes, and lengthy construction timetables, cities are often challenged to deliver the results that communities demand as quickly as they would like. Interim design strategies are tools and tactics that cities can use to improve their roadways and public spaces in the near term. They include low-cost, interim materials, new public amenities, and creative partnerships with local stakeholders, which together enable faster project delivery and more flexible and responsive design.

Interim Design Strategies

Whether setting a parklet along a curb, pedestrianizing a narrow corridor, or redesigning a complex intersection, cities have the opportunity and the responsibility to make the most efficient use of valuable street space. An interim design can serve as a bridge to the community, helping to build support for a project and test its functionality before going into construction.

Activating the Curb

While the separation of the street and the sidewalk is generally defined through on-street parking, street furniture, and physical elements that buffer pedestrians from motorists, curbsides have the potential to host a wide variety of uses beyond parking.

On-street parking spaces or curb-side travel lanes may be converted to bus lanes or cycle tracks. Two to four parking spaces can be replaced

with a parklet or bike corral. On weekends or at lunchtime, curbsides can host food trucks or vendors that activate street life and create a destination within the street.

Interim Sidewalk Widening

As neighborhoods change and develop, the intensity of a street's uses may also change. Sidewalks can be expanded using interim materials, such as epoxied gravel, planter beds, and bollards, easing pedestrian congestion in advance of a full reconstruction.

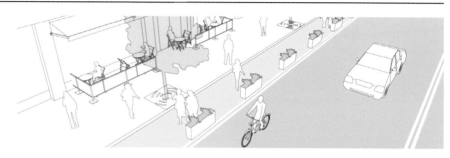

Traffic Calming

Temporary traffic calming devices may be installed using a narrow drainage channel. These offset islands help slow speeds in advance of a full reconstruction.

Bike Corral

Bike corrals typically replace one parking space at the request of a local business or property owner and accommodate 12–24 bikes. Corrals can be installed at corners to daylight an intersection since bicycle parking has no effect on the visibility of pedestrians to moving vehicle traffic. Bike corrals have been shown to have a positive impact on business.[1]

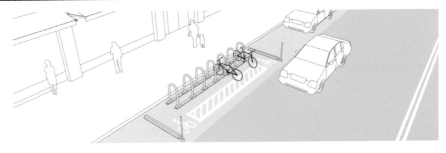

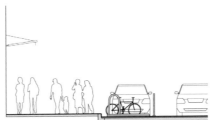

Bike Share

Bike share stations can serve as an integral part of the public transit system. Station maps and kiosks can serve as a focal point that orients tourists and visitors while drawing people to key destinations.

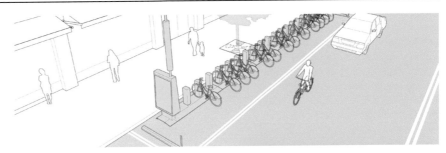

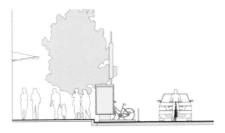

Parklet

Parklets are public seating platforms that replace several parking spaces. They serve as a gathering place for the community and can energize local stores and shops.

From Pilot to Permanent

The conventional project development process proceeds from plan to capital construction over a number of years, during which momentum and funding for the project may fade. From a project's conceptualization to its actual implementation, a lot can change in terms of political will, citizen involvement, and prevailing city policies. While many of these processes are designed to assess and evaluate the potential impacts of a project, small-scale, interim changes—wider sidewalks, public plazas, street seating—can deliver results to communities more quickly. Interim design strategies allow cities to assess the impacts of their intended project in real time and realize their benefits faster than typical processes allow. While a majority of these interim designs go on to become full-scale capital projects, some are altered or redesigned in the process based on how they perform in real time. This results in a better final product and saves on future expenditures and improvements that need to be made in revision.

While interim design strategies can be effective and instrumental toward realizing certain projects, they may not be appropriate at all locations or for all communities. Cities should assess how an interim design will be received by local stakeholders in order to avoid derailing a project that might have been better received in its capital phase.

While many cities have branded the interim design as a pilot or test phase for a project, others view the design as equivalent to a permanent reconstruction. The level of permanence depends on the individual project, but should always be communicated at the outset.

	CONVENTIONAL PROJECT DEVELOPMENT	PHASED/INTERIM DESIGN STRATEGY
Year 1	Concept	Concept
	Plan/Outreach	Plan/Outreach
Year 2		Interim Installation
		Impacts Analysis
Year 3	Design	Design
Year 4		
Year 5	Construction	Construction

WILLOUGHBY PLAZA, BROOKLYN

Before
A low-volume, 1-block stretch of Willoughby Street in downtown Brooklyn served as a popular corridor for pedestrians between Brooklyn's civic center and main shopping district.

Interim
This segment was closed to vehicle traffic using temporary planters, seating, and bollards in 2006.

After
Following a full capital construction process, Willoughby Plaza was made permanent and officially opened in 2013.

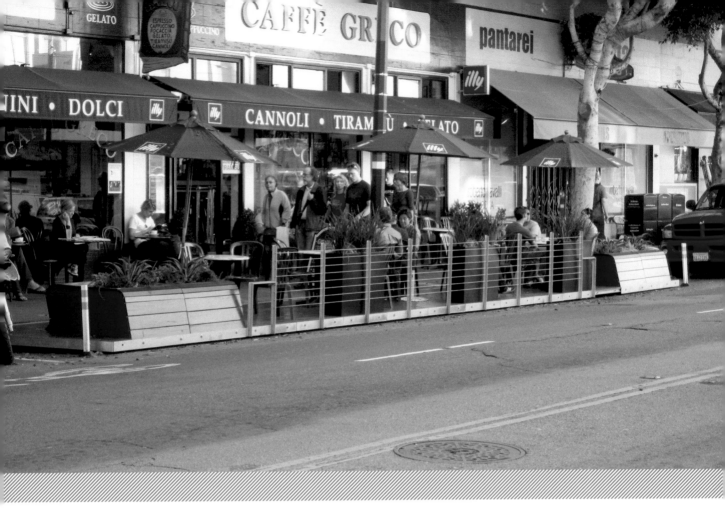

Parklets

Parklets are public seating platforms that convert curbside parking spaces into vibrant community spaces. Also known as street seats or curbside seating, parklets are the product of a partnership between the city and local businesses, residents, or neighborhood associations. Most parklets have a distinctive design that incorporates seating, greenery, and/or bike racks and accommodate unmet demand for public space on thriving neighborhood retail streets or commercial areas.

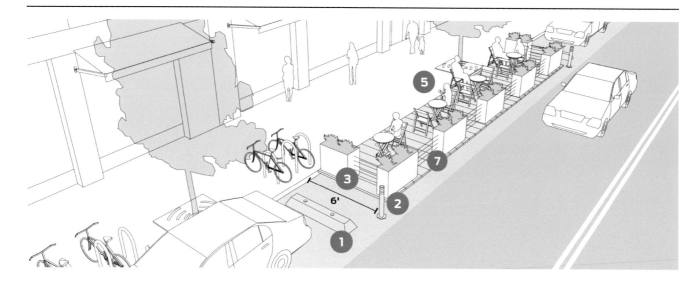

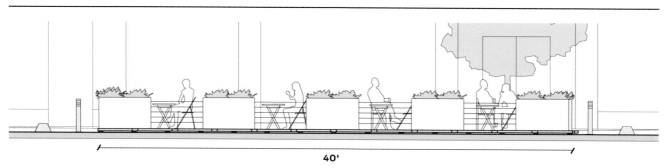

APPLICATION

Parklets are typically applied where narrow or congested sidewalks prevent the installation of traditional sidewalk cafes or where local property owners or residents see a need to expand the seating capacity and public space on a given street. To obtain a parklet, property owners enter into an agreement with the city, in some cases through a citywide application process, procuring curbside seating in place of one or more parking spaces.

BENEFITS & CONSIDERATIONS

Parklets are typically administered through partnerships with adjacent businesses and/or surrounding residents. Partners maintain and program the parklet, keeping it free of trash and debris. Where no local partners are present, a parklet may be installed and managed by the city as a traditional park or public space.

Parklets can be managed through a competitive application process by a city transportation, planning, or public works agency.[1]

Cities with frequent snowfall should consider the removal of parklets during the winter to prevent conflicts with plows and street cleaning vehicles.

Costs vary based on the design and size of the parklet. Design and installation costs are generally assumed by the maintenance partner. Standardized parklet designs may be made available by the city to make the program more appealing and affordable.[2]

While parklets are foremost intended as assets for the community, their presence has also been shown to increase revenues for adjacent businesses.[3]

CRITICAL

1 To ensure visibility to moving traffic and parking cars, parklets must be buffered using a wheel stop at a desired distance of 4 feet from the parklet. This buffer may also serve as a space for adjacent property owners to accommodate curbside trash collection.

2 Parklets should have vertical elements that make them visible to traffic, such as flexible posts or bollards.

Wheel stops on either side of the parklet.

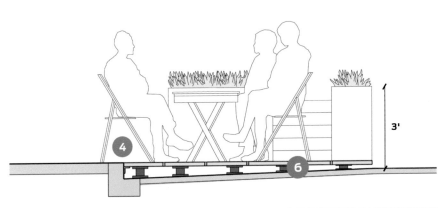

3'

A steel transition plate ensures a flush transition from the curb to the wooden parklet surface.

Bison pedestals are a popular substructure for parklets.

LOCATION: PHILADELPHIA, PA
Before, during construction, and after—parklet on 44th Street.

3 Parklets have a desired minimum width of 6 feet (or the width of the parking lane). Parklets generally entail the conversion of one or more parallel parking spaces or 3–4 angled parking spaces, but may vary according to the site, context, and desired character of the installation. Where a parklet stretches the length of an entire curb, accessibility and sightlines must be taken into account.

The design of a parklet should not inhibit the adequate drainage of stormwater runoff. Small channels between the base and the platform facilitate drainage.

4 Parklets should have a flush transition at the sidewalk and curb to permit easy access and avoid tripping hazards.

RECOMMENDED

Parklets should avoid corners and are best placed at least one parking space away from the intersection corner. Where installation of a parklet is under consideration for a site near an intersection, volumes of turning traffic, sightlines, visibility, and daylighting should be taken into account.

Parklets should be heavy enough to make theft impossible or unlikely. Site selection should consider the level of surveillance both during the day and at night.

5 Incorporate seating into the parklet. Seating may be integrated into the design itself or made possible with moveable tables and chairs.

6 Designs for the substructure of a parklet vary and depend on the slope of the street and overall design for the structure. The substructure must accommodate the crown of the road and provide a level surface for the parklet. "Bison pedestals" spaced under the surface and of different heights are a common application. Another method is to provide steel substructure and angled beams.[4]

Parklets should use a slip-resistant surface to minimize hazards and should be accessible to wheelchair users.

Parklet floor load-bearing weight standards vary by agency. At a minimum, design for 100 pounds per square foot.[5]

7 Include an open guardrail to define the space. Railings should be no higher than 3 feet and be capable of withstanding at least 200 feet of horizontal force.[6]

Parklet siting should avoid obstructing underground utility access and electrical transformer vaults.

OPTIONAL

The design of any individual parklet may vary according to the wishes of the primary partner or applicant. Designs may include seating, greenery, bicycle racks, or other features, but should always strive to become a focal point for the community and a welcoming public gathering place. Cities may opt to have a standard design template to reduce design and construction costs for applicants.

Bicycle parking may be incorporated into or adjacent to the parklet.

SAN FRANCISCO PARKLET PROGRAM

San Francisco's Parklet Program converts parking spots into vibrant public spaces. Parklets extend the sidewalk and provide neighborhood amenities like seating, landscaping, bike parking, and art. Through an application process that requires documented neighborhood support, the program allows the community to actively participate in the beautification and creative use of the public realm. Designs are accessible and inclusive, inviting pedestrians, bicyclists, and shoppers to linger, relax, and socialize. Each parklet has a distinct, site-specific design that reflects the neighborhood's unique character,

Process

Each year, an interagency team, led by the San Francisco Planning Department, issues requests for parklet proposals. Storeowners, community organizations, business improvement districts, residents, and nonprofit institutions may apply to sponsor a parklet. Sponsors must conduct community outreach, design the parklet, fund its construction, undertake maintenance, and supply liability insurance. Materials and designs must be temporary and removable, and sponsors must renew parklet permits annually.

Design

San Francisco's parklets generally meet the following design requirements:

- Replace 1–2 parallel, or 3 perpendicular or diagonal parking spaces.

- Be sited on streets with speed limits of 25 mph or less and slopes below 5 percent.

- Have no interference with utility access, fire hydrants, disabled parking, bus zones, or curbside drainage.

- Meet construction standards of both the San Francisco Building Code and the Americans with Disabilities Act Accessibility Guidelines.

- Include wheel stops, reflective elements at corners, and a buffered edge.

- Incorporate high-quality, durable materials.

Privately sponsored and funded, parklets represent an economical means of expanding and energizing public space. Since the program's initial 2010 launch with 6 pilot parklets, San Francisco has installed 38 parklets across the city.

Temporary Street Closures

Temporary streets closures, such as play streets, block parties, street fairs, and open streets, demonstrate the range and diversity of ways in which a city's streets may be utilized. Whether done as a precursor to a future project or as a seasonal or weekly event, temporary closures can activate the street and showcase participating businesses and communities. Depending on a street's usage and characteristics, temporary street closures can take multiple forms, ranging from an emphasis on active recreation, biking, or exercise to business activity, food, or arts.

DISCUSSION

Temporary street closures allow cities to take better advantage of their roadways, especially at off-peak hours and weekends.

Closures call attention to neighborhood businesses and destinations and increase foot traffic on designated corridors. Data collection can support public perceptions of the success of a temporary implementation and may be especially helpful toward creating a permanent public space.[1]

When themed around active recreation and exercise, temporary street closures may be aligned with a city's larger public health goals and encourage residents to take advantage of parkways and boulevards as recreational amenities.[2]

Closures typically require additional trash pickup and street cleaning in the evening or the following day to ensure that local residents and businesses remain active and supportive.

CRITICAL

A removable traffic control device or barrier should be used to ensure that vehicles do not encroach on a street closure. Police enforcement is not necessary or desirable in all cases.

RECOMMENDED

Where regularly scheduled, especially if daily or weekly, a regulatory sign should be posted to indicate the closure.

Closures are most successful when programmed with events and activities throughout the day. Programs may include performances, seating, food stalls, and other activities.[3]

ATLANTA, GA

Street furniture, including chairs, tables, and lighting, can help to activate a closed pedestrian street.

On days of closure, loading and unloading should be permitted for local businesses in the morning and evening hours.

Naming conventions for temporary pedestrian streets should be carefully considered. Branding should be analyzed based on the intended audience and participants.

BRONX, NY

"Weekend Walks" is a 5-year-old program provided by NYC DOT and local partnering organizations. The program provides community street events throughout the city from May to October.

OPTIONAL

For certain streets, night closures may be desirable. Night closures should be more closely monitored and protected from traffic due to the potential lack of visibility for drivers. Extra lighting may be required and police enforcement is recommended at night.

NEW ORLEANS, LA
Bourbon Street closes every night, year-round.

Bicyclists may be permitted to ride through temporary street closures in certain cases. Typically, shared use by bicycles should be determined based on anticipated pedestrian traffic as well as a street's available width. Bicyclists should always be permitted to ride through "open streets" events. (See table at right.)

TYPES OF CLOSURES

Temporary street closures restrict a street to pedestrians—and in some cases bicyclists, rollerbladers, and skateboarders—at specific times of day, specific days of the week or during the year, or for certain seasons. While many streets are periodically closed to traffic for special events, temporary street closures refer to streets with a regularly scheduled closing, such as a pedestrian street, play street, or farmers market.

Temporary street closures are often applied in the following scenarios:

Play Street
Low-volume, local streets closed for a specific portion of the afternoon and/or weekend for play and recreation, play streets are often adjacent to playgrounds, schools, or residential areas with limited park space in the vicinity.

Pedestrian Street
Pedestrian streets are typically held either on weekends or seasonally on neighborhood main streets. They are based around cultural and community programming and events, rather than commercial activity or street food.

Market
Streets adjacent to public parks, landmarks, or along key corridors that are fully or partially closed for a food fair or farmers market. Markets are often seasonal and open only during daylight hours.

Open Streets
Major boulevards or parkways closed on weekends for a specific set of hours. Open streets typically include pedestrians, bicyclists, and other recreational users, as well as limited static activities near the curbside.

LOS ANGELES'S CICLAVIA INITIATIVE

Los Angeles's CicLAvia initiative opens city streets to bicyclists, pedestrians, skateboarders, and rollerbladers, temporarily transforming the city's largest public space, its streets, into major active transportation corridors. Initially conceived by a group of volunteers in 2008, CicLAvia will soon hold its 7th annual event. Routes have ranged between 6.3 and 15 miles, with the most recent CicLAvia drawing an estimated crowd of 150,000.

Public-Private-Nonprofit Partnership

Drawing inspiration from ciclovias in Latin America, a group of volunteers began conceptualizing a Los Angeles version of the event in 2008. After incorporating as a nonprofit in 2009, CicLAvia staff visited neighborhood council meetings to build support and demonstrate community interest. With an energized constituency behind them, CicLAvia teamed up with the Mayor's Office and the Los Angeles Department of Transportation (LADOT) to plan logistics for the event. The resulting public-private-nonprofit partnership benefits all stakeholders. The nonprofit sets the overall vision for CicLAvia, holds liability insurance, and fundraises for the event. Funding stems from

a mix of government grants, foundation dollars, and private sponsorships. A private production company manages logistics, graphic design, and staffs the events. The LADOT and the Mayor's Office coordinate traffic management, permits, and policy.

Design

Route selection for the CicLAvias looks at population density, transit connections, commercial corridors, and destinations, such as parks, plazas, or notable buildings. Planners typically avoid streets with steep grades and work with city staff to patch potholes and provide a smooth surface along the designated route. Each CicLAvia tries to use a new route to showcase different neighborhoods in Los Angeles, though staff have also found a benefit to repeating routes, especially as they build relationships with businesses and test more creative ways of engaging with participants.

CicLAvias remain permeable to motorists at designated crossing points, minimizing disruption to the transportation network and reducing the potential for road closures that isolate one half of the city from the other. LADOT's Special Traffic Operations Division, which handles events, produces a traffic management plan for each CicLAvia, detailing intersection modifications, roundabouts, and other temporary

infrastructure designs that will manage the traffic flow of participants and remove conflict points. CicLAvia staff are responsible for implementing the plan from LADOT.

Permits

Using the city's *Street Closure Provisions and Application Procedures* for guidance, CicLAvia applies for permits before each event. Through a conditional exception, CicLAvia does not need 51% approval from neighbors to close a street, but instead must post an informational flyer to every business and residence along the route in advance of a CicLAvia.

Community Engagement

In advance of every CicLAvia event staff canvas the route to inform business owners and residents of the upcoming street closure, including what to expect and how to participate. LADOT policy requires parked cars to be moved from the route for public safety reasons. Prior to each event, CicLAvia staff alert motorists to the parking restriction to avoid cars being towed. Los Angeles Bike Coalition volunteers assist with this large-scale community engagement effort.

Interim Public Plazas

Interim public plazas transform underutilized areas of roadway into public spaces for surrounding residents and businesses. Using low-cost materials, such as epoxied gravel, movable planters, and flexible seating, interim public plazas reconfigure and revitalize intersections that might otherwise be unsafe or underutilized.

Like parklets, interim public plazas are the result of a successful partnership between the city and a neighborhood group or business association. Partners maintain, oversee, and program the space. While many public plazas proceed from an interim phase to final reconstruction within 3–5 years, the intermediate application allows the community to build support for and benefit from the public space in the near term, before major capital construction.

APPLICATION

Interim public plazas are most commonly applied under the following circumstances:

- A dedicated partner, typically a business or neighborhood association, or a community with unmet demand for public space, wants to activate, program, and take ownership of an underutilized road space and can maintain it throughout the year.

- An underutilized street segment has low vehicle traffic, pedestrian demand is unmet, and foot traffic is overflowing into the roadway.

- Safety or operational issues with existing traffic call for a temporary reconfiguration of the intersection.

- Funds have been allocated to the permanent installation of a plaza, but capital implementation remains several years away.

SAN FRANCISCO, CA

BENEFITS & CONSIDERATIONS

Public plazas have the potential to:

- Make intersections safer, more compact, and easier to cross for pedestrians.

- Slow traffic speeds and mitigate potentially dangerous intersection conflicts.

- Activate a public place by reclaiming space unused or underused by motorists.

- Energize surrounding streets and public spaces, creating foot traffic that can boost business and invigorate street life in a neighborhood.[1]

CRITICAL

1 Parking shall not be allowed or permitted within the public plaza. Parking may be maintained adjacent or parallel to the plaza, but should be designed along the footprint of the future capital implementation.

2 Interim public plazas shall be constructed with ADA-compliant tactile warning strips at the crosswalks. Extra attention should be paid to how sight-impaired individuals will navigate these spaces.

Stripe a double white line along the edge of the plaza to legally prohibit vehicles from entering the space.

RECOMMENDED

Plazas should be defined using low-cost, durable materials, such as epoxied gravel, paint, and thermoplastic.[2] Climate factors into the selection of specific materials and their long-term durability.

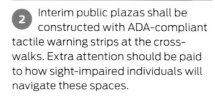

NEW YORK, NY
Coordinated designs using flexible chairs, tables, and planters define interim public spaces throughout New York City's five boroughs.

3 Plazas should be designed with a strong edge and defined using a combination of striping, bollards, and larger fixed objects, such as granite rocks and/or planters.

Prior to implementation of a public plaza, cities are advised to post an informational placard advertising the plaza to ensure that local stakeholders are aware of the installation.

Tables and seating may be movable to permit flexible use of the space and to limit costs. Whether or not to secure seating at night should be determined by the maintenance partner.[3]

Corners and other areas of a plaza subject to encroachment by errant or turning vehicles should be reinforced using heavy objects and bollards that alert drivers of the new curb line.

Adequate lighting should be provided at plazas at all times of day.

OPTIONAL

4 Heavy planters, granite blocks, moveable seating, and other street furniture elements may be incorporated into the interim design.

BROOKLYN, NY
Granite blocks help define the edge of a new plaza.

LOS ANGELES, CA

Bicycle parking may be installed in coordination with the installation of a temporary plaza.

Art installations, performances, vendors, and markets can improve the quality and identification of a public plaza, while engaging local artists, communities, and business owners.

Plazas should be designed to accommodate freight loading and unloading where access to the curb is required at early morning hours for adjacent businesses.

Drainage should be considered in the design of the pilot plaza. Sites should have minimal cross slope or be designed using edge treatments that mitigate the overall slope.

NEW YORK CITY PLAZA PROGRAM

The New York City Department of Transportation's (NYC DOT) Plaza Program converts underutilized road space into neighborhood amenities through partnerships with local nonprofit organizations and communities. The program, launched in 2008, is currently in its sixth round of applications and has realized 22 new public spaces for New Yorkers.

Community Partnerships

The Plaza Program accepts proposals from community-based nonprofit organizations to create neighborhood plazas through an annual competitive application process. NYC DOT funds plaza design and construction and incorporates community input through public visioning workshops. The non-profit partner is responsible for conducting community outreach, participating in design meetings, formulating a funding plan, providing insurance for the plaza, undertaking maintenance, and programming activities and events to ensure that the plaza becomes a vibrant neighborhood destination. Locally known and respected neighborhood nonprofits bring on-the-ground insight and

expertise and help NYC DOT secure approval from the local community board, an essential milestone in realizing any plaza project.

Design

The Plaza Program generally involves capital reconstruction, though NYC DOT now awards more funding for projects that initially use interim materials, such as moveable tables, planters, and umbrellas. Interim materials give plazas a degree of flexibility—assuaging opponents, streamlining the design and construction process, using funding more efficiently, and allowing community members to enjoy the plaza's benefits sooner. Once interim plazas are in place, local support for permanent construction tends to grow. Whether permanent or temporary, using standard materials simplifies work for NYC DOT operations crews.

Funding

Dedicated, long-term funding for the Plaza Program was secured through PlaNYC 2030, New York City's long-range plan released in 2007. PlaNYC set a goal to ensure all New Yorkers live within a ten-minute walk of a park, and the Plaza Program helps fulfill that goal.

Intersections

For city streets to meet the needs and demands of everyone using them, intersections—both large and small—need to function as safely and efficiently as possible. Good intersection design, however, goes beyond making streets safer. Well-designed intersections use street space to bring people together and invigorate a city, while making traffic more intuitive, seamless, and predictable for those passing through.

Intersection Design Principles

Whether while driving, shopping, walking, or lingering, intersections are a focal point of activity and decision, and thus are critical parts of the city streetscape and transportation network. Intersections account for the most serious conflicts between pedestrians, bicyclists, and drivers, but also present opportunities to reduce crashes when designed carefully. Good intersection design can tap civic and economic potential, infusing overbuilt or underutilized spaces with street life.

Intersection design should facilitate visibility and predictability for all users, creating an environment in which complex movements feel safe, easy, and intuitive. Their design should promote eye contact between all street users, engendering a streetscape in which pedestrians, drivers, and bicyclists are aware of one another and can effectively share space.

Principles

Intersections are the most challenging aspect of street design in an urban environment. Capacity constraints at these pinch points in the roadway network govern the width of roadways as they pass through them. People on foot may avoid difficult crossings or subject themselves or their children to considerable risks while crossing a street at a poorly designed intersection. The principles outlined here enable practitioners to build intersections as meeting points that function well for everyone using them.

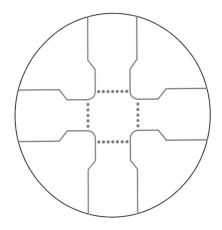

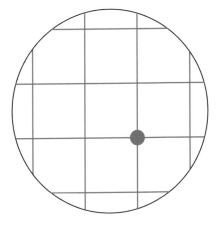

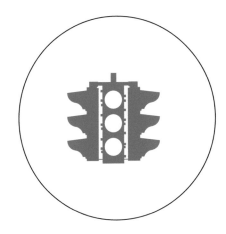

Design Intersections to Be as Compact as Possible

Compact intersections reduce pedestrian exposure, slow traffic near conflict points, and increase visibility for all users. Limit the addition of dedicated turn lanes and pockets, and remove slip lanes where possible. Break large, complex intersections into a series of smaller intersections. Use existing pedestrian behaviors and desire lines to dictate design.

Analyze Intersections as Part of a Network, not in Isolation

Solutions may be found at the corridor or network level. Tradeoffs can often be made between the intersection and the network in terms of traffic volume and capacity.

Integrate Time and Space

Reconfiguring intersections in time (through signalization) provides an alternative to widening intersections to solve delay or congestion. Integrate spatial and temporal intersection design strategies throughout a project.

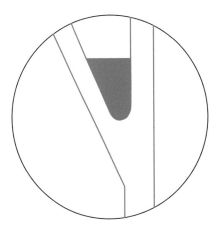

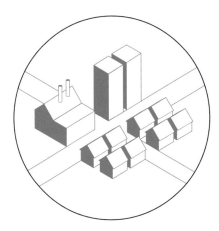

Intersections Are Shared Spaces

The goal of intersection design is not strictly to reduce the number of conflicts for a given user at a select location, but to create a space in which users are mutually aware of one another and visible and predictable in their actions to reduce the overall rate and severity of crashes.

Utilize Excess Space as Public Space

Interim public plazas and low-cost safety improvements should be used to enhance public life and mitigate safety concerns in the near term.

Design for the Future

Design should account for existing and future land uses as well as projected and induced demand for all users. Land uses and pedestrian generators play an equally important role in making decisions about intersections and relate directly to the desires and objectives of the surrounding community.

Major Intersections

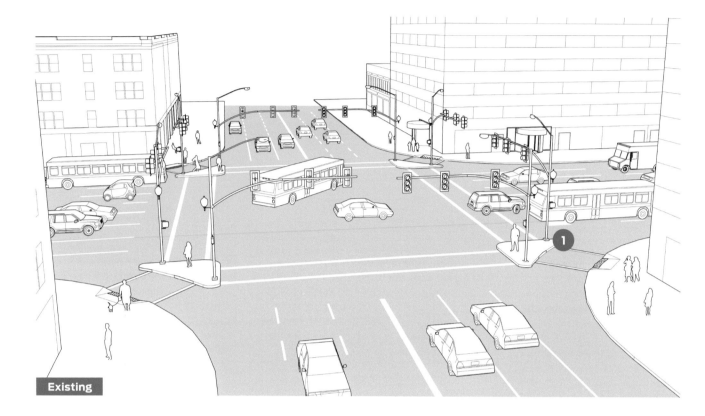

Existing

The intersection of 2 major streets can act as both a barrier and a node. Redesigning major intersections requires designers to critically evaluate the tools and tradeoffs available to make an intersection work better for everyone. While shorter cycle lengths, compact design, and pedestrian safety islands are all desirable components of a multi-modal intersection, the tradeoffs inherent in each make these difficult to achieve simultaneously. Weigh intersection geometry, signal timing, and traffic volumes to formulate a design that clarifies the hierarchy of street users, while enhancing the safety and legibility of the intersection.

EXISTING CONDITIONS

1 Large intersections like that shown above are often over-designed and difficult for both motorists and pedestrians to manage. Channelized right turns and other features create unsafe, high-speed turns.

Evaluate whether or not all travel lanes are absolutely necessary through corridor analysis, and assess the impact of removing a lane in the traffic network.

At large intersections, bicyclists and pedestrians suffer from long exposure times and multileg crossings. Cycle lengths of 120 seconds or more and 2-stage crossings further exacerbate delay. Large corner radii and inadequate pedestrian safety islands designed to accommodate high-speed turns fail to convey safety within a busy intersection.

RECOMMENDATIONS

Minimize unused space. Excess pavement increases speed and accommodates driver error. Control speeds by tightly managing the design and spatial layout of intersections. Tighten lane widths and eliminate unnecessary travel lanes, reallocating space for bike lanes and cycle tracks.

2 Use leading pedestrian intervals (LPI) to give pedestrians a head start entering the crosswalk. Add pedestrian safety islands where possible and eliminate channelized right-turn lanes to slow turn speeds and create self-enforcing yielding to pedestrians. Provide a right-turn pocket or mixing zone where right-turn volumes merit. Minimize speed, especially at turns. Curb extensions, tight corner radii, cycle tracks, and pedestrian safety islands force drivers to navigate intersections cautiously.

Reconstruction

3 At large intersections, accommodate bicyclists either through full signalization or mixing zones. While a dedicated bicycle signal is generally desirable from a safety point of view, an added signal phase lengthens the overall cycle length and exacerbates delay for all users. Avoid the use of mixing zones or restrict turns where turn volumes are likely to make bicyclists feel unsafe.

4 Bicyclist left turns may be facilitated using intersection crossing markings and a 2-stage turn queue box.

Align lanes through an intersection and enforce turning lanes with curb extensions to reduce merging and weaving. Delineate guide markings through intersections to reduce conflicts and guide turning vehicles.

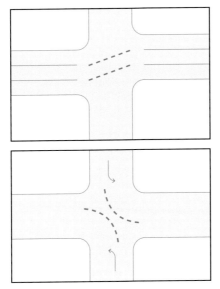

5 Consider banning left or right turns where they are problematic or create safety conflicts.

Provide left-turn pockets where frequent left turns are made, retaining a 6-foot pedestrian safety island by reducing the bike lane buffer.

6 Minimize delay to transit vehicles using transit signal priority. Determine the transit stop placement based upon the location of major destinations, transfer activity, and route alignment. At signalized and unsignalized intersections, far-side transit stops are preferable. Bus bulbs improve transit travel times and provide a dedicated space for waiting passengers.

Daylight intersections to maximize sight distance. Reduce vehicle speeds to match sight distance, rather than enlarging the intersection or removing obstructions.

Intersections of Major and Minor Streets

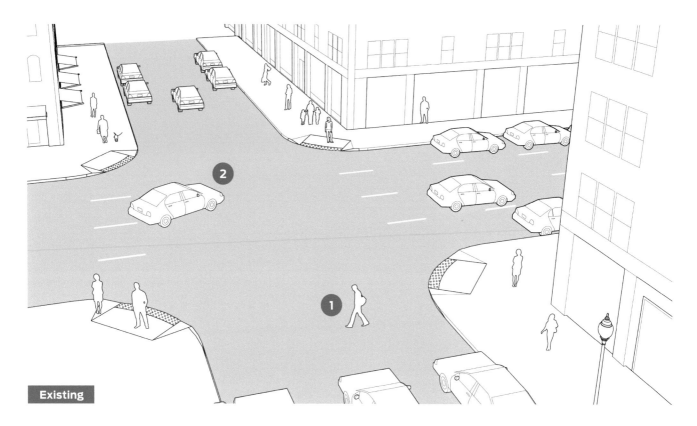

Existing

Intersections of major and minor streets often lack the same level of definition, safety, and clarity as major intersections. Bicyclists and pedestrians, though legally permitted to cross at these locations, are implicitly discouraged from doing so through design. Vehicles often fail to yield at these locations and have few design cues to suggest they should.

Where major streets meet minor streets, define the transition in street type and context using "gateway" treatments such as curb extensions, raised crossings, and tight curb radii. Use design elements so that people turning from the major to the minor street become aware they are entering a slow-speed environment.

EXISTING CONDITIONS

The illustration above shows a typical intersection of a minor street with a major through street or collector. The low-volume minor approach is unsignalized while the major corridor has high speeds, making it difficult to cross the street.

1 The traffic on the major street discourages pedestrian and bicycle crossings. Crosswalks and signage are lacking at the minor street, failing to alert motorists to potential cross traffic.

2 Cars turn at high speeds onto the minor street, compromising the slow-speed, residential environment.

Crossing major streets can be intimidating for many pedestrians, especially where insufficient gaps in traffic make crossings risky and no striping or signage exists to alert motorists.

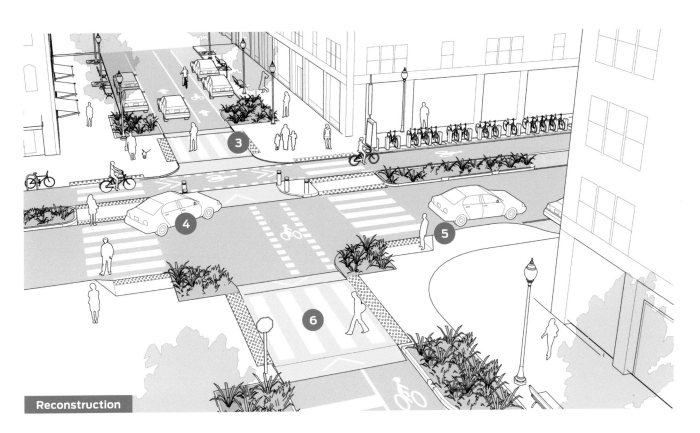

Reconstruction

RECOMMENDATIONS

Evaluate intersection volumes to ensure that there are sufficient gaps in traffic for an unsignalized, marked crossing. Look at the overall traffic network to balance permeability while minimizing cut-through traffic. Do not restrict bicycle or pedestrian crossings of major roads, even if warrants are not met.

3 Use raised crossings and curb extensions to limit turning speeds from the major to the minor street. Raised crossings increase visibility and the potential for a vehicle to yield to a crossing pedestrian. When crossing a minor street, a raised cycle track can be carried through an intersection and be combined with a raised crosswalk to clarify and accentuate priority.

4 Minimize turning speeds from the major to the minor street. Design so that drivers on the major street yield to people in the crosswalk and cycle track. Ensure that drivers on the minor street can turn onto or cross the major street without excessive delay (either caused by signals or traffic). Bollards at legal turns keep turning drivers off the crosswalk and reduce crashes with pedestrians.

5 If a signal is used, shorten cycle lengths and coordinate signal timing to ensure routine gaps in traffic. Otherwise, pedestrians may try to cross on a red signal with a gap in the vehicle platoons. Long, unsignalized corridors may require the installation of all-way stop signs.

6 Stripe crosswalks at unsignalized crossings and critically evaluate whether or not pedestrians may benefit from enhanced crossing treatments, such as safety islands, high-visibility signage, actuated beacons, or full signalization.

Raised Intersections

Raised intersections create a safe, slow-speed crossing and public space at minor intersections. Similar to speed humps and other vertical speed control elements, they reinforce slow speeds and encourage motorists to yield to pedestrians at the crosswalk.

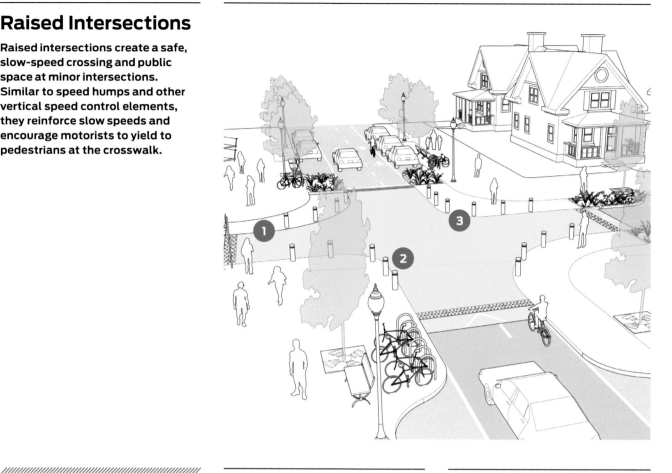

RECOMMENDATIONS

1 Raised intersections are flush with the sidewalk and ensure that drivers traverse the crossing slowly. Crosswalks do not need to be marked unless they are not at grade with the sidewalk. ADA-compliant ramps and detector strips are always required.

2 Bollards along corners keep motorists from crossing into the pedestrian space. Bollards protect pedestrians from errant vehicles.

3 Where two 1-way streets intersect, there will be two corners around which no drivers turn. This can be designed with the smallest constructible radius (approximately 2 feet) as long as a 40-foot fire truck can make the turn without encroaching upon the sidewalk.

Neighborhood Traffic Circles

Neighborhood traffic circles lower speeds at minor intersection crossings and are an ideal treatment for uncontrolled intersections. They may be installed using simple markings or raised islands, but are best applied in conjunction with plantings that beautify the street and the surrounding neighborhood. Careful attention should be paid to the available lane width and turning radius used with traffic circles.

RECOMMENDATIONS

1 Neighborhood traffic circles have been shown to increase safety at intersections. Crosswalks should be marked to clarify where pedestrians should cross and that they have priority.[1] ADA-compliant ramps and deflector strips are required.

2 Shared-lane markings or inter-section-crossing markings guide bicyclists through the intersection. Where a bicycle boulevard turns at a minor intersection, use bicycle way-finding route markings and reinforce route direction using shared-lane markings.

3 A neighborhood traffic circle on a residential street is intended to keep speeds to a minimum. Provide approximately 15 feet of clearance from the corner to the widest point on the circle.

4 Shrubs or trees in the circle further the traffic calming effect and beautify the street, but need to be properly maintained so they do not hinder visibility.

Complex Intersections

Complex intersections, especially those situated at neighborhood centers or at the junction of several major streets, have tremendous potential to fulfill latent demand for public space. Irregular intersections, which result from successive urban developments and alterations, often occur at the threshold between adjacent grids or where new or preexisting roads cut through the conventional neighborhood layout. Often overbuilt and confusing, these intersections present safety hazards to all users. Traffic flow and multiphase signals result in

long delays for pedestrians and cyclists, while at the same time causing confusion among drivers. Acute angled intersections reduce visibility for motorists, while obtuse intersections allow for high-speed turns. Both acute- and obtuse-angled intersections create unnecessarily long pedestrian crossings. Redesign intersections as close to 90 degrees as possible, implementing turn restrictions and street reversals where applicable.

The following examples are all based on actual intersections.

Y-Intersection
Add island or square-off. Limit turning speed around obtuse angles; shorten crossings; separate vehicle flows.

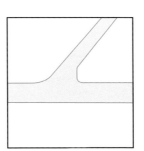 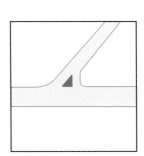 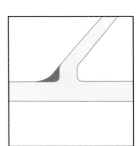

X-Intersection
Minimize footprint or create two mini-intersections. Mini-junctions need to be far enough apart to operate as two or close enough to operate as one.

 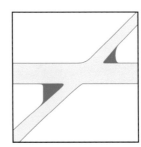 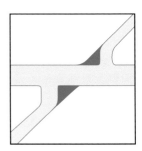

Five-Way
Square off and separate, or remove a leg. Some streets are ideal to serve as non-motorized routes.

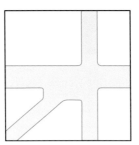 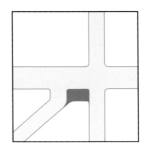 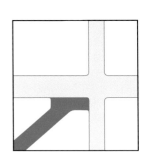

Grid Plus Circle
Prioritize either grid or circle. Maintain view corridor.

Y Plus Grid
Add island or square off. Limit turning speed around obtuse angles; shorten crossings; separate vehicle flows.

  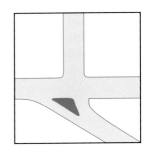

Small and Large
Use curbs to manage drivers. Extend medians.

Grid Plus Large
Clarify and simplify. Convert redundant streets into greenswards.

  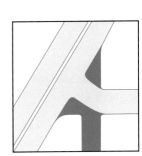

Large Ends
Organize and prioritize flows. Solution might be found in the network.

 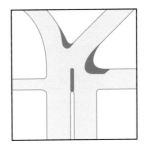 

Complex Intersection Analysis

The following design process takes a sample complex intersection and details how to understand its existing function, analyze its movements, identify opportunities, and create a new design. Driving this process is the underlying need to let land use, community desires, and usage determine solutions.

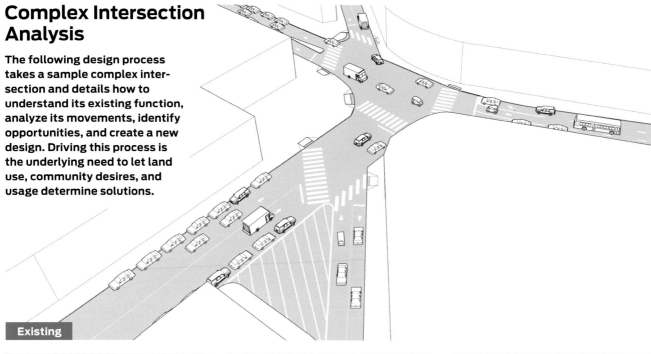

Existing

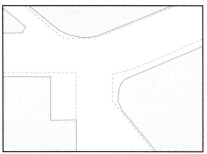

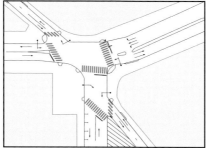

CONTEXT

Understand the context within which the intersection functions. Analyze the intersection's urban-design qualities and document specific gathering places, landmarks, transit stations, and other drivers of activity. Engage the public in this process, allowing safety concerns and community visions to drive the ultimate redesign. Document static conditions, such as:

· Land use
· Property lines and setbacks
· Building footprints, arcades, and courtyards
· Building entrances, façades, and view corridors
· Bridges, tunnels, and unique structures
· Parks, plazas, and public spaces
· Transit stations
· Topography, grading, and stormwater flows

GEOMETRY, SIGNALS, SIGNS, & MARKINGS

Survey the intersection's dynamic conditions, or how people are meant to move through the junction based upon existing markings. These elements include:

· Curbs
· Curb ramps and driveways
· Street furniture, plantings, tree pits, benches, and bus shelters
· Centerline of street
· Lane markings: number of lanes, geometry, direction
· Crosswalks
· Stop lines/advanced stop lines
· Traffic signals
· On-street and off-street parking
· Bicycle infrastructure

VEHICLE VOLUMES

Map vehicle movements and turns to understand how motorists are using the intersection. Overlay volume data to illustrate the relative importance of each movement, looking for low volume turning movements in particular.

This process does not need to be data intensive or time consuming. Transportation agencies typically have access to volume and signalization data. Pair this with observation and understanding of the local planning context and how the street fits into the overall traffic network.

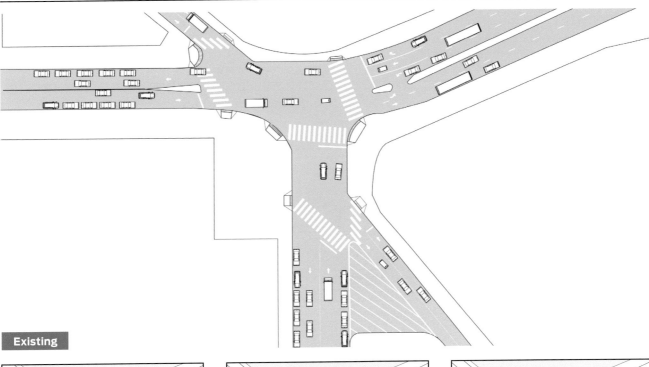

Existing

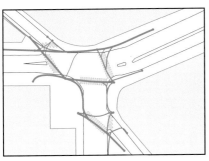

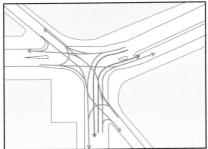

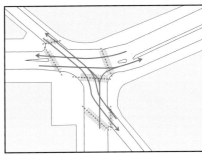

PEDESTRIAN ACTIVITY

Document how pedestrians use and activate the intersection as a public space. Where are people gathering, sitting, and talking? What activities are they engaged in? Which public spaces attract people and which do not?

Overlay how pedestrians actually move through the junction and the volumes of those movements. Where do people actually cross the street? How many people? In what direction? In this case, a train station is located at the northeast corner of the study area and attracts large volumes of people on foot. In urban locations with continual activity, this step can often be accomplished by 15–30 minutes of observation.

TRANSIT & BICYCLE ACTIVITY

Assess the volume and movement of cyclists as part of the planned and existing cycling network. Document bus headways and volumes, as well as the placement and location of bus stops.

SIGNALIZATION

If there is a traffic signal, plot the phases to show how the intersection flows. Obtain phasing data from the appropriate agency, or, if phasing data is not available, the general timing plan can be ascertained with a stopwatch. Note whether pedestrian and vehicle signals are fixed or actuated. Observe how well the phases match volumes, how people comply, and when signals give priority to drivers, cyclists, or pedestrians. Note the tradeoffs made in giving more time or protected signal phases to particular modes or movements. Does adding a protected left-turn phase for vehicles reduce the available crossing time for pedestrians across the side street and encourage crossing against the walk signal?

Redesign

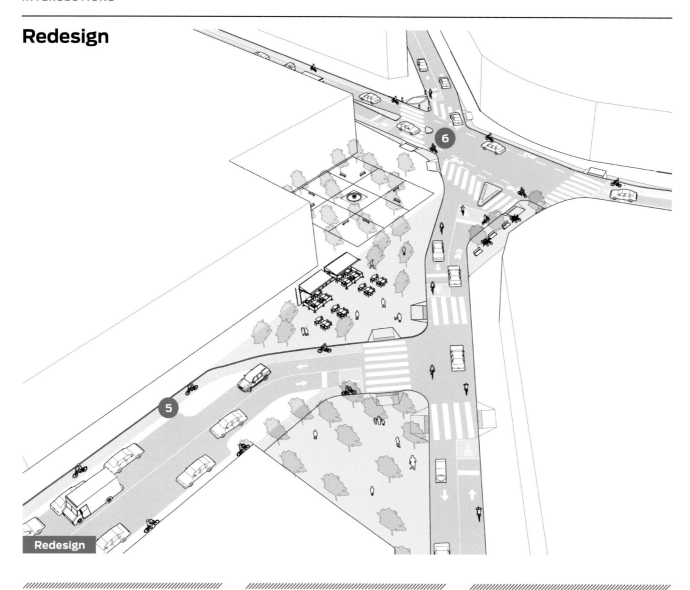

Redesign

CLARITY

1 Break complex intersections into multiple compact ones. Bend streets so that they meet at as close to a right angle as possible.

Maintain view corridors and sight lines for legibility and wayfinding.

2 Mirror turn lanes with curb extensions and medians.

3 Align stop lines at all legs of the intersection to be perpendicular to the travel lanes, enhancing overall clarity and visibility for both vehicles and pedestrians.

COMPACTNESS

4 Minimize intersection size through the addition of curb extensions and medians.

Minimize vehicle turning speeds using medians, realignment, and tight curb radii.

MULTI-MODAL

5 Reallocate space for bicyclists and pedestrians. Widen narrow sidewalks and add cycle tracks.

Realign crosswalks to meet the pedestrian desire line.

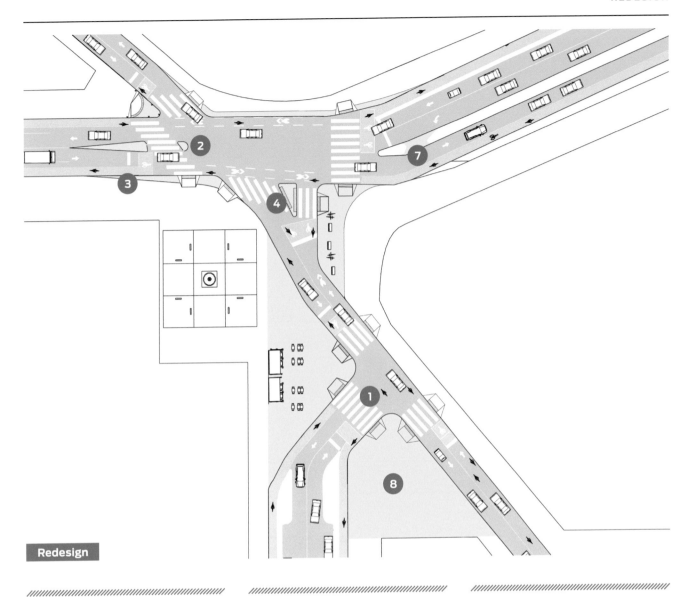

Redesign

CONFLICT REDUCTION

Restrict vehicle turns at acute-angled intersections with very low volumes.

6 Add median tips at crosswalks.

Consolidate driveways to properties with multiple entry points.

7 Close openings in medians that interfere with intersection operations.

RIGHT SIZING

Where traffic-volume data reveals excess vehicle capacity, reduce the number of lanes along a corridor, consolidate excess turn lanes, and eliminate slip lanes. Reallocate space to medians, bicycle infrastructure, or sidewalks.

PUBLIC SPACE

8 Utilize excess asphalt from the reconfiguration to create a public plaza. Low-cost materials may be used on an interim basis until full reconstruction and curb relocation. Evaluate the performance of the new configuration and adjust the design as necessary.

Assess and design the entire public realm in a holistic way to create one seamless pedestrian realm. Integrate intersection design elements with the surrounding buildings and plazas. Enhance and take advantage of existing public spaces in the redesign area.

NEW YORK, NY

Unveiled in 2010 as part of a series of major reconfigurations along Manhattan's Broadway corridor, Union Square embodies the key principles used by NYC DOT in redesigning complex intersections. As part of the redesign, multiphase traffic signals were simplified, pedestrian plazas created at undefined or underused locations, and bikeways and turn lanes added to better accomodate southbound traffic.

Intersection Design Elements

Intersections are a critical aspect of street design, the point where motorist, bicycle, and pedestrian movements converge. Successful intersection design addresses all mobility and safety goals as well as opportunities to enhance the public realm. This section explores intersection design and operation, from signal timing to crosswalks, and investigates each concept as it relates to citywide goals for safety, mobility, and more vibrant, accessible public spaces.

Crosswalks and Crossings

Safe and frequent crosswalks support a walkable urban environment. Crosswalks should be applied where pedestrian traffic is anticipated and encouraged. While application of crosswalk markings alone is not a viable safety measure in all situations, crosswalks benefit and guide pedestrians, while reinforcing their right-of-way at intersections.

Pedestrians are especially sensitive to minor shifts in grade and geometry, detours, and the quality of sidewalk materials and street lighting. Crosswalk design has the potential to both shape and respond to pedestrian behaviors and demands, while guiding people toward the safest possible route.

Crosswalks

DISCUSSION

As traffic speeds and volumes increase, so too does the level of protection desired by pedestrians. Where vehicle speeds and volumes are high and pedestrian access is expected at regular intervals, signalized crossings preserve a safe walking environment. Where anticipated pedestrian traffic is low or intermittent, or where vehicle volumes are lower and pedestrian crossings shorter, designers may consider the use of unsignalized crossing treatments such as medians, hybrid or rapid flash beacons, or raised crossings.

On streets with low volume (<3,000 ADT), low speeds (<20 mph), and few lanes (1–2), marked crosswalks are not always necessary at the intersections. At schools, parks, plazas, senior centers, transit stops, hospitals, campuses, and major public buildings, marked crosswalks may be beneficial regardless of traffic conditions.

On streets with higher volume (>3,000 ADT), higher speeds (>20 mph), or more lanes (2+), crosswalks should be the norm at intersections.

Designers should take into account both existing and projected crossing demand. Frequent crossings reinforce walkability and have the potential to fuel greater demand. Where signalized or stop-controlled pedestrian crossings are not warranted but demand exists or is anticipated, designers should continue to work toward goals of safety and comfort for people walking through other means, such as actuated crossings or enhanced crossing treatments.

Judgment on the application of a crosswalk should be based on multiple factors, including land uses, present and future demand, pedestrian compliance, speed, safety, and crash history. Volumes alone are not enough to determine whether or not a particular device should be used.

REDMOND, WA

The presence of a crosswalk does not, in and of itself, render a street safe. Based on their surrounding contexts, speed, and overall roadway width, crosswalks often require additional safety measures such as safety islands, signals, or traffic calming.

While pedestrians generally have the right to cross at any intersection regardless of crosswalks, designers should be sensitive to the misperception that a crosswalk is the only legal place to cross the street. Use crosswalks as both a guide for pedestrians and a way to communicate crossings to motorists.

The practice of discouraging pedestrian crossings by leaving uncontrolled crossings unmarked is not a valid safety measure. Instead, it encourages unsafe, risk-taking behavior and discourages walking citywide. Efforts should be made to enhance or highlight desired crossings wherever practicable. Hybrid beacons, rapid flash beacons, raised crossings, medians, and other safety countermeasures may be suitable and less expensive than full signalization. These should all be considered before leaving an uncontrolled crossing unmarked.

CRITICAL

All legs of signalized intersections must have marked crosswalks unless pedestrians are prohibited from the roadway or section thereof, or if there is no actual pedestrian access on either corner and no likelihood that access can be provided. Pedestrians are unlikely to comply with a 3-stage crossing and may place themselves in a dangerous situation as a result.

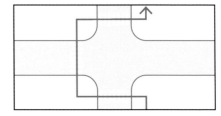

Pedestrians are frustrated by and often do not comply with 3-leg intersection crossings.

NO PEDESTRIANS (MUTCD 2B.36, R5-10c, or R9-3a) signs should not be used unless they are accompanied by a physical barrier and positive information about where pedestrians should cross the street.

SAN FRANCISCO, CA

ST LOUIS, MO

ORLANDO, FL

Pedestrian countdown signals create a more predictable crossing environment and give adequate warning to pedestrians attempting to cross a roadway. All new crosswalk signals should include pedestrian signals with countdowns.

Pedestrian crossings should be at grade except in instances where they are crossing limited-access highways. Pedestrian overpasses and underpasses pose security risks from crime and are frequently avoided for a more direct (if less safe) crossing.

Pedestrian noncompliance increases with relative detour and delay. Delays exceeding 40 seconds at signalized crosswalks and 20 seconds at unsignalized or yield-controlled crosswalks may cause risk-taking behavior. Countdown signals and shorter cycle lengths can help to increase compliance, and may be paired with other strategies.

RECOMMENDED

Map the pedestrian network and crossing locations to understand how it corresponds to the bicycle, transit, and vehicle networks. Pedestrians interact with the environment at a fine-grained level and have frequent demand for accessing destinations.

Locate pedestrian crossings as per current or projected pedestrian desire lines. Balance their placement with that of the auto traffic network, so as not to severely compromise either. There is no absolute rule for crosswalk spacing. Rather, it depends on block length, street width, building entrances, traffic signals, and other factors. 120-200 has been shown to be sufficient.

Pedestrians, including elderly and disabled persons, should be able to cross an intersection in a single cycle, rather than two cycles, unless a street is segmented by a transit, bus, or other destination median.

Channelized turning "porkchop" islands are not recommended and should be avoided. Turning traffic often fails to yield to pedestrians crossing at these locations.

OPTIONAL

Crosswalk spacing criteria should be determined according to the pedestrian network, built environment, and observed desire lines. In general, if it takes a person more than 3 minutes to walk to a crosswalk, wait to cross the street, and then resume his or her journey, he or she may decide to cross along a more direct, but unsafe or unprotected, route. While this behavior depends heavily on the speed and volume of motorists, it is imperative to understand crossing behaviors from a pedestrian's perspective.

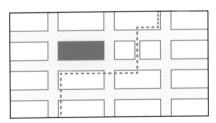

Pedestrian networks are fine-grained, including frequent midblock desire lines and destinations.

Conventional Crosswalks

Crosswalks should be designed to offer as much comfort and protection to pedestrians as possible. Historically, many crosswalks were designed using inadequate, narrow striping, setbacks, deviations from the pedestrian walkway, and considerable crossing distances.

Intersection crossings should be kept as compact as possible, facilitating eye contact by moving pedestrians directly into the driver's field of vision.

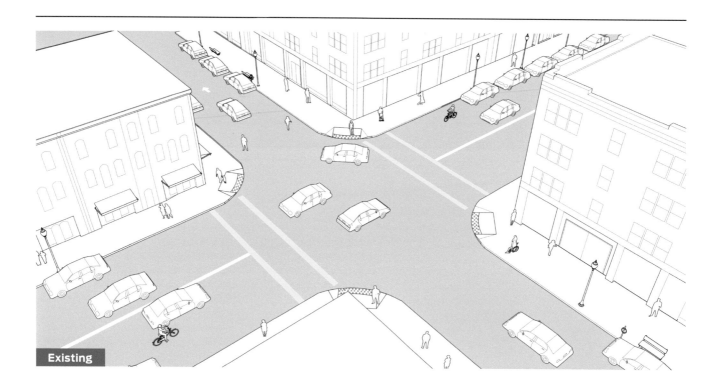

Existing

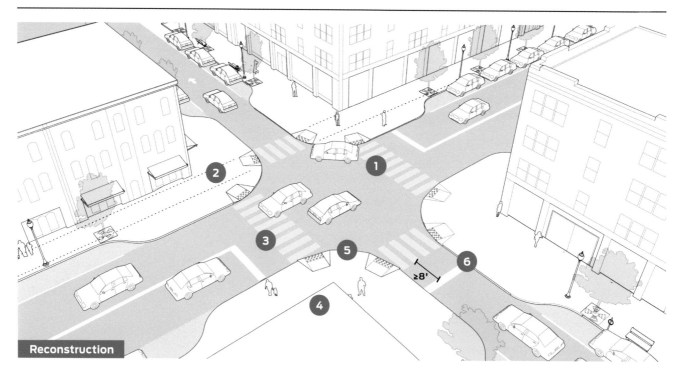

≥8'

Reconstruction

CRITICAL

1 Stripe all signalized crossings to reinforce yielding of vehicles turning during a green signal phase. The majority of vehicle-pedestrian incidents involve a driver who is turning.

2 Stripe the crosswalk as wide as or wider than the walkway it connects to. This will ensure that when two groups of people meet in the crosswalk, they can comfortably pass one another. Crosswalks should be aligned as closely as possible with the pedestrian through zone. Inconvenient deviations create an unfriendly pedestrian environment.

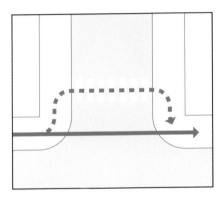

3 High-visibility ladder, zebra, and continental crosswalk markings are preferable to standard parallel or dashed pavement markings. These are more visible to approaching vehicles and have been shown to improve yielding behavior.

Street lighting should be provided at all intersections, with additional care and emphasis taken at and near crosswalks.

4 Accessible curb ramps are required by the Americans with Disabilities Act (ADA) at all crosswalks.

RECOMMENDED

5 Keep crossing distances as short as possible using tight corner radii, curb extensions, and medians. Interim curb extensions may be incorporated using flexible posts and epoxied gravel.

6 An advanced stop bar should be located at least 8 feet in advance of the crosswalk to reinforce yielding to pedestrians. In cases where bicycles frequently queue in the crosswalk or may benefit from an advanced queue, a bike box should be utilized in place of or in addition to an advanced stop bar.

Stop bars should be perpendicular to the travel lane, not parallel to the adjacent street or crosswalk.

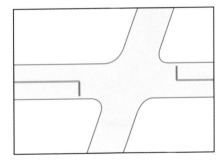

OPTIONAL

Right-turn-on-red restrictions may be applied citywide or in special city districts and zones where vehicle-pedestrian conflicts are frequent. Right-turn-on-red restrictions reduce conflicts between vehicles and pedestrians.

Midblock Crosswalks

Midblock crosswalks facilitate crossings to places that people want to go but that are not well served by the existing traffic network. These pedestrian crossings, which commonly occur at schools, parks, museums, waterfronts, and other destinations, have historically been overlooked or difficult to access, creating unsafe or unpredictable situations for both pedestrians and vehicles. Designers should study both existing and projected pedestrian volumes in assessing warrants for midblock crossings to account for latent demand.

Existing

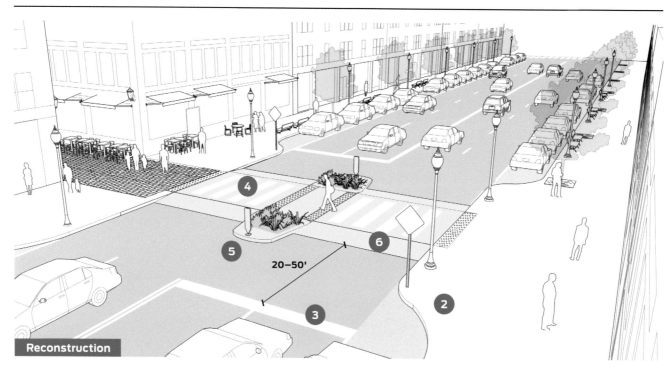

Reconstruction

RECOMMENDED

1 Install a midblock crosswalk where there is a significant pedestrian desire line. Frequent applications include midblock bus stops, metro stations, parks, plazas, building entrances, and midblock passageways.

Vertical elements such as trees, landscaping, and overhead signage help to identify crosswalks and islands to drivers.

2 Daylighting in advance of a crosswalk makes pedestrians more visible to motorists and cars more visible to pedestrians. This may be accomplished by restricting parking and/or installing a curb extension.

3 Stop lines at midblock crossings should be set back 20–50 feet. This ensures that a person crossing the street is visible to the second driver when the first driver is stopped at the stop line.

4 Stripe the crosswalk, regardless of the paving pattern or material. Otherwise, drivers are not likely to see it, especially at night.

5 Medians or safety islands create a 2-stage crossing for pedestrians, which is easier and safer.

6 At key access points to parks, schools, and waterfronts, and at .intersections with local streets, raised crossings increase visibility, yielding behavior, and create a safer pedestrian crossing environment.

Where an unsignalized crossing exists at a transit stop, enhanced crossing treatments or actuated signals should be added. Transit stops should ideally be located so that pedestrians cross behind the bus or transit vehicle. Far-side stop placement is preferable to near side or midblock placement and increases the visibility of pedestrians crossing behind the bus.

LOS ANGELES, CA

OPTIONAL

A pedestrian tracking survey may be used to document where and how people cross a street, complex intersection, or plaza. This information is useful in locating crosswalks and safety islands, redesigning intersections, and understanding the interface between streets and the surrounding buildings and public spaces.

Actuated pedestrian signals (half-signals), hybrid beacons, or rapid flash beacons may be considered at greenway crossings, midblock locations, or unsignalized crossings where infrequent crossings make a traffic signal or stop sign unnecessary. Fixed-time signals or passive detection are preferable to push-button detection.

Unsignalized midblock crosswalks may be applied at locations with inconsistent pedestrian demand or where a pedestrian connector intersects midblock with a small- or medium-sized roadway

Unsignalized crossings should be highlighted using additional warning signage, high-visibility lighting and markings, actuated beacons (where applicable), and traffic calming features, such as raised crossings and midblock curb extensions.

Where midblock pedestrian crossings in a low-volume downtown commercial or neighborhood residential area are frequent, a designer may consider the application of a shared street treatment. Shared streets should have limited or no markings to reinforce the regulation of the street as a shared space.

Pedestrian Safety Islands

A pedestrian safety island reduces the exposure time experienced by a pedestrian in the intersection. While safety islands may be used on both wide and narrow streets, they are generally applied at locations where speeds and volumes make crossings prohibitive, or where three or more lanes of traffic make pedestrians feel exposed or unsafe in the intersection.

CHICAGO, IL

2 lanes

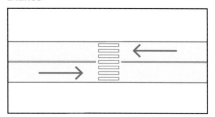

3 lanes

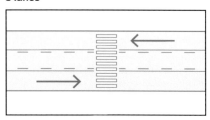

4 lanes

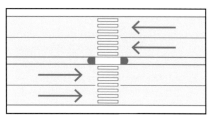

As the number of travel lanes increases, pedestrians feel more exposed and less safe entering the intersection. For unsignalized crossings, higher speeds and volumes may necessitate the use of a median at narrower cross sections.

DISCUSSION

Pedestrian safety islands limit pedestrian exposure in the intersection. They are recommended where a pedestrian must cross three lanes of traffic in one direction (on a 1-way or a 2-way street), but may be implemented at smaller cross-sections where space permits.

CRITICAL

Pedestrian safety islands should be at least 6 feet wide, but have a preferred width of 8–10 feet. Where a 6-foot-wide median cannot be attained, a narrower raised median is still preferable to nothing. The minimum protected width is 6 feet, based on the length of a bicycle or a person pushing a stroller. The refuge is ideally 40 feet long.

The cut-through or ramp width should equal the width of the crosswalk. Where this cannot be achieved, crosswalks should be striped wider than the cut-through area.

RECOMMENDED

All medians at intersections should have a "nose" which extends past the crosswalk. The nose protects people waiting on the median and slows turning drivers.

Safety islands should include curbs, bollards, or other features to protect people waiting.

It is preferable to have the crosswalk "cut-through" the median. Where the median is wider than 17 feet, ramps are preferred. This dimension is based on a 6-inch-high curb, two 1:12 ramps, and a 5-foot-wide level landing in the center.

OPTIONAL

Pedestrian safety islands may be enhanced using plantings or street trees. Plantings may require additional maintenance responsibilities and need to be maintained to ensure visibility.

CRYSTAL CITY, VA
The "nose" in the median above protects pedestrians from turning cars.

Corner Radii

Corner radii directly impact vehicle turning speeds and pedestrian crossing distances. Minimizing the size of a corner radius is critical to creating compact intersections with safe turning speeds. While standard curb radii are 10–15 feet, many cities use corner radii as small as 2 feet. In urban settings, smaller corner radii are preferred and actual corner radii exceeding 15 feet should be the exception.

DISCUSSION

The size of the corner relates directly to the length of the crosswalk. Longer crosswalks take more time to cross, increasing pedestrian exposure risk and diminishing safety.[1]

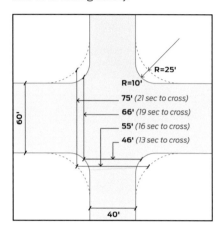

A smaller curb radius expands the pedestrian area, allowing for better pedestrian ramp alignment.

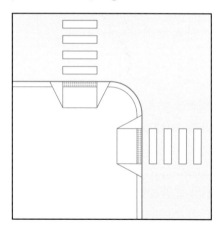

A large corner radius should not be used to facilitate a truck turning from the right lane into the right lane.[2]

Effective Turning Radius

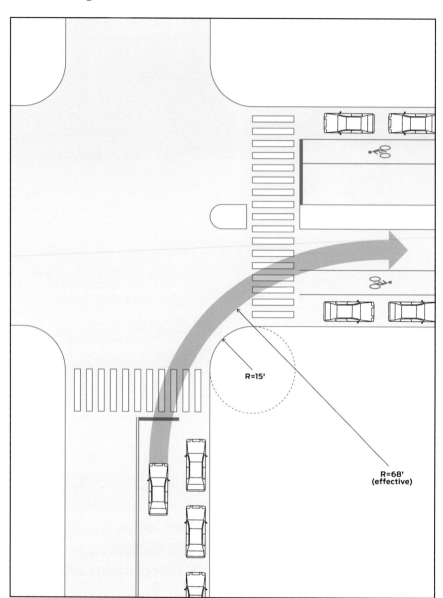

The distinction between the corner radius and the effective turning radius is crucial and often overlooked. The corner radius may be a simple or a complex curve and depends primarily on the presence of on-street parking, bike lanes, the number of travel lanes, medians, and traffic control devices.

Designers often determine corner radii based on the intersection geometry only and overlook the effective radius. As a result, drivers making a turn on a green signal have little incentive to turn into the nearest receiving lane and routinely turn as wide as possible to maintain travel speeds.

RECOMMENDED

Turning speeds should be limited to 15 mph or less. Minimizing turning speeds is crucial to pedestrian safety, as corners are where drivers are most likely to encounter pedestrians crossing in the crosswalk.[3]

Minimize effective turning radius where possible by employing one or more of the following techniques:

· Select the smallest possible design vehicle.

· Accommodate trucks and buses on designated truck and bus routes.

· Restrict right-turns-on-red so there is no expectation of turning into the nearest receiving lane.

· Require larger vehicles to employ on-roadway personnel to "spot" vehicles through difficult turns.[4]

· Design so that emergency vehicles may utilize the full area of the intersection for making turns.

OPTIONAL

In cases where the curb radius of a given intersection has resulted in an unwieldy or unsafe crossing distance, but where funding is not available to reconstruct the curb immediately, a city may delineate the appropriate curb radius using interim materials such as epoxied gravel, planters, and bollards. This should be a temporary option until funding becomes available for a more permanent treatment.[5]

HONOLULU, HI

This landscaped island reduces corner and effective radii while maintaining existing drainage and providing a cut-through for pedestrians.

Various methods that accommodate large vehicles, while restricting the turning speed of smaller vehicles, may be used to avoid unnecessary widening of the intersection.

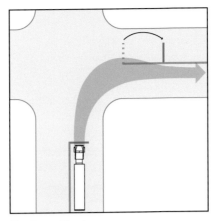

Stop bar set back

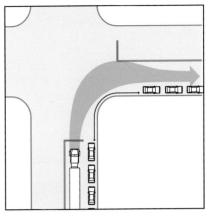

Parking restrictions near the corner

Narrower streets with curbside travel lanes may require larger corner radii because the effective turning radius mirrors the actual corner radius. The same holds true for streets with curb extensions. Streets should not be designed with larger corner radii in anticipation of the entire roadway being used for vehicle traffic at some point in the future.

TURNING SPEED

The formula for calculating turning speed is:

$$R = \frac{V^2}{15\,(.01E + F)}$$

R = Centerline turning radius (effective)

V = Speed in miles per hour (mph)

E = Super-elevation. This is assumed to be zero in urban conditions.

F = Side friction factor

Turning Speed & Radius Reference Chart[6]

V (MPH)	E	F	R (FT)
10	0	0.38	18
15	0	0.32	47
20	0	0.27	99
25	0	0.22	174

Source: American Association of State Highway and Transportation Officials. *A Policy on Geometric Design of Highways and Streets*. Washington D.C.: 2011; Formula 3-8.

Visibility/ Sight Distance

Visibility and sight distance are parameters central to the inherent safety of intersections, driveways, and other potential conflict points. Intersection design should facilitate eye contact between street users, ensuring that motorists, bicyclists, pedestrians, and transit vehicles intuitively read intersections as shared spaces. Visibility can be achieved through a variety of design strategies, including intersection "daylighting," design for low-speed intersection approaches, and the addition of traffic controls that remove trees or amenities that impede standard approach, departure, and height sight distances. Sight line standards for intersections should be determined using target speeds, rather than 85th-percentile design speeds. This prevents wide setbacks and designs that increase speeds and endanger pedestrians.

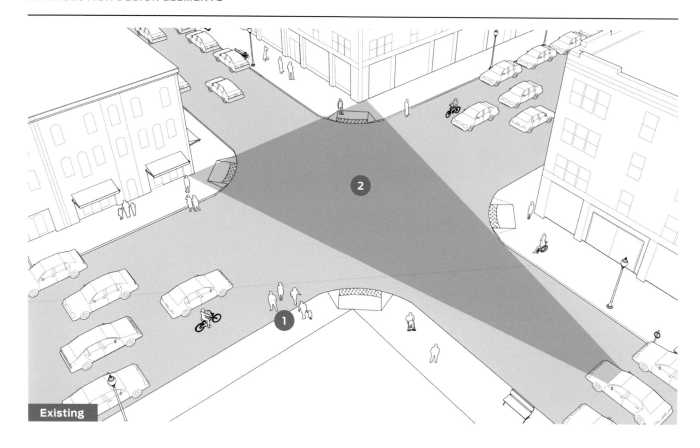

Existing

Lower speeds at urban intersections with insufficient sight distances. Low speeds yield smaller sight triangles, meaning that drivers can focus on less activity and better react to potential conflicts.

DISCUSSION

Visibility is impacted by the design and operating speed of a roadway. Determining sightlines based on existing or 85th-percentile speeds is not sufficient in all cases. Designers need to proactively lower speeds near conflict points to ensure that sightlines are adequate and movements predictable, rather than widening the intersection or removing sightline obstacles.

Sight triangles required for stopping and approach distances are typically based upon ensuring safety at intersections with no controls at any approach. This situation rarely occurs in urban environments, and occurs only at very low-speed, low-volume junctions. At uncontrolled locations where volume or speed present safety concerns, add traffic controls or traffic calming devices on the intersection approach.[1]

SAN FRANCISCO, CA
While this uncontrolled intersection operates at low speeds, it may still benefit from stop control or traffic calming.

1 In urban areas, corners frequently act as a gathering place for people and businesses, as well as the locations of bus stops, bicycle parking, and other elements. Design should facilitate eye contact between these users, rather than focus on the creation of clear sightlines for moving traffic only.

2 Wide corners with large sight triangles may create visibility, but in turn may cause cars to speed through the intersection, losing the peripheral vision they might have retained at a slower and more cautious speed.

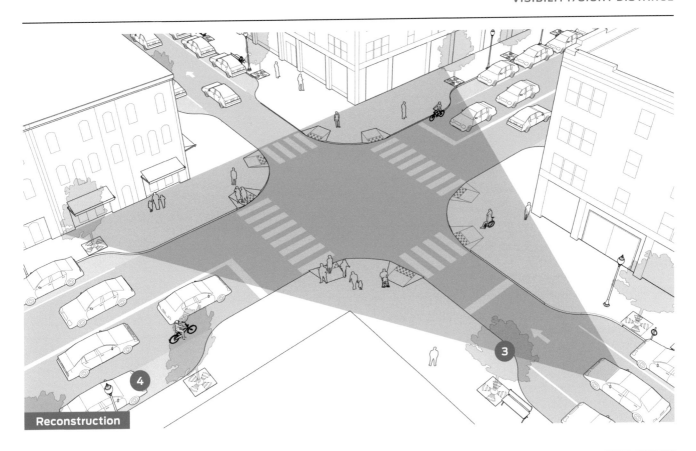

Reconstruction

Intersections with insufficient visibility should be reconstructed to be more compact. Compact intersections place more activity within the sight triangle, giving all users a better view of potential conflicts.

In certain circumstances, an object in the roadway or on the sidewalk may be deemed to obstruct sightlines for vehicles in a given intersection and to pose a critical safety hazard. Removal of the object in question is a worst-case scenario based on significant crash risk and crash history. Many objects, such as buildings, terrain features, trees in historic districts, and other more permanent parts of the landscape should be highlighted using warning signage and other features, rather than removed.

CRITICAL

In determining the sight distance triangle for a given intersection, use the target speed, rather than the design speed, for that intersection.

3 Fixed objects, such as trees, buildings, signs, and street furniture, deemed to inhibit the visibility of a given intersection and create safety concerns, should not be removed without the prior consideration of alternative safety-mitigation measures, including a reduction in traffic speeds, an increase in visibility through curb extensions or geometric design, or the addition of supplementary warning signs.

Traffic control devices must be unobstructed in the intersection, and shall be free of tree cover or visual clutter.

RECOMMENDED

4 Daylight intersections by removing parking within 20–25 feet of the intersection.[2]

ATLANTA, GA
Street trees enhance the public realm and are often sited close to intersections without inducing safety concerns.

Site street trees at a 5-foot minimum from the intersection, aligning the street tree on the near side of the intersection with the adjacent building corner. Street trees should be sited 3 feet from the curb return and 5 feet from the nearest stop sign.[3]

Lighting is crucial to the visibility of pedestrians, bicyclists, and approaching vehicles. Major intersections and pedestrian safety islands should be adequately lit with pedestrian-scaled lights to ensure visibility. In-pavement flashing lights can enhance crossing visibility at night, but should be reinforced by well-maintained retro-reflective markings.[4]

ST. LOUIS, MO
Pedestrian-scale lighting illuminates the sidewalk and adjacent storefronts.

OPTIONAL

Additional signage may be provided to enhance visibility at a given intersection, but should not replace geometric design strategies that increase visibility.

BOULDER, CO
Signage, in combination with a raised crosswalk, improves visibility at this right-turn lane.

Traffic Signals

Equally important to the allocation of space, in the form of street cross-sections and geometry, is the allocation of time, performed by traffic signals. Space and time, in combination, govern how streets operate and how well they provide mobility, safety, and public space. Signal timing is an essential tool, not just for the movement of traffic, but also for a safer environment that supports walking, bicycling, public transportation, and economic vitality.

Signalization Principles

The operation of a traffic control system should closely mirror a city's policy goals and objectives. Managing traffic signals is important because signals directly impact the quality of the transportation system. While geometric enhancements to a corridor may demarcate space for bikes and buses and create a more multi-modal cross-section, signal timing influences delay, compliance, safety, and mode choice. Traffic signal timing that provides insufficient time for someone to cross the street, for instance, is likely to create an unpleasant experience and may discourage walking entirely. Likewise, significant delays may cause street users to violate the traffic signal or take unsafe risks entering intersections.

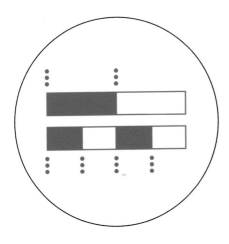

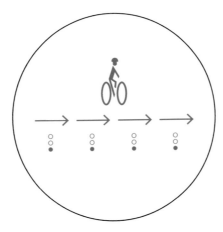

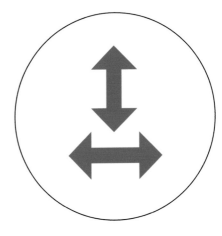

Shorten Signal Cycles to Increase Turnover

Short signal cycle lengths minimize delay in a complex network environment, reducing wait times in all directions and creating crossing opportunities at closer intervals. Avoid simultaneously adding multiple turn lanes and increasing turn phase intervals. Do one or the other, but not both.

Prioritize Walking, Bicycling, and Transit

Use signal priority tools, such as leading pedestrian intervals, synchronized signals for bicycles, or transit signal priority along corridors with established or desired modal priority.

Keep the Number of Signal Phases to a Minimum

While separating traffic through signal phasing may have safety benefits, additional phases increase wait times for everyone by increasing the overall length of the signal cycle. Consider turn restrictions at dangerous intersections or, where turn volumes necessitate a dedicated turn phase, introduce a protected left-turn phase.

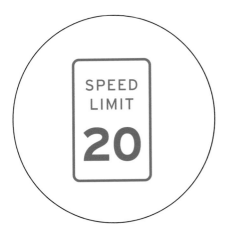

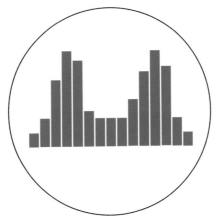

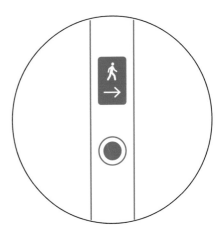

Time Signals to the Speed You Intend Traffic to Go

Synchronize signals at or below the target speed to maintain safe vehicular travel speeds and discourage speeding, especially on 1-way streets.

Adjust Timing for Peak and Off-Peak Volumes

Signal timing should be managed for both peak and off-peak volumes. Timing may be adjusted to meet different levels of activity throughout the day.

Use Fixed-Time Signals as Opposed to Actuated Signals

Fixed, rather than actuated, signals are preferable in urban areas to increase the predictability of the urban environment and ensure consistent opportunities for pedestrian crossings and cross traffic.

Leading Pedestrian Interval

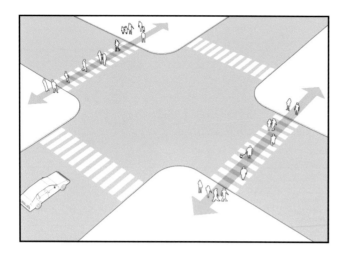

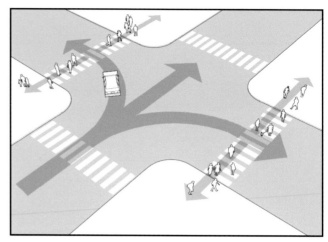

PHASE 1
Pedestrians are given a minimum head start of 3–7 seconds when entering the intersection.

PHASE 2
Through and turning traffic are given the green light. Turning traffic yields to pedestrians already in the crosswalk.

APPLICATION

A Leading Pedestrian Interval (LPI) typically gives pedestrians a head start of 3–7 seconds when entering an intersection with a corresponding green signal in the same direction of travel. LPIs enhance the visibility of pedestrians in the intersection and reinforce their right-of-way over turning vehicles, especially in locations with a history of conflict.

Use LPIs at intersections where heavy turning traffic comes into conflict with crossing pedestrians during the permissive phase of the signal cycle. LPIs are typically applied where both pedestrian volumes and turning volumes are high enough to warrant an additional dedicated interval for pedestrian-only traffic.

BENEFITS & CONSIDERATIONS

LPIs increase the visibility of crossing pedestrians and give them priority within the intersection.

LPIs have been shown to reduce pedestrian-vehicle collisions as much as 60% at treated intersections.[1]

LPIs typically require adjustments to existing signal timing that are relatively low in cost compared to other countermeasures.

CRITICAL

LPIs are critical at intersections where heavy right- or left-turning volumes create consistent conflicts and safety concerns between vehicles and pedestrians.

RECOMMENDED

LPIs should give pedestrians a minimum head start of 3–7 seconds, depending on the overall crossing distance. Intervals of up to 10 seconds may be appropriate where pedestrian volumes are high or the crossing distance is long.

To increase the effectiveness of an LPI and improve visibility of pedestrians at high-conflict intersections, install a curb extension at the intersection.

OPTIONAL

Where a bikeway on the through movement conflicts with turning traffic, use a leading bicycle interval along with the leading pedestrian interval. A leading bicycle interval clears the intersection of all cyclists quickly and can help prevent right hook collisions.

Protected Left Turn Phasing and Restrictions

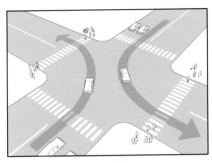

PROTECTED LEFT TURN PHASING

At locations where left turning motorists pose a significant safety threat to through traffic, pedestrians, and bicyclists, left turns can be given a protected phase.

APPLICATION

Protected left-turn phasing is most often applied in the following situations:

- Intersections with history of collisions between left-turning and through vehicles, potentially resulting from geometric constraints or heavy conflicting volumes;
- at locations where pedestrians or cyclists may experience risk associated with left turning traffic relying on the acceptance of gaps;
- and where a large skew at an intersection poses a serious risk to oncoming vehicles or pedestrians and may be functionally enhanced through separation.

BENEFITS & CONSIDERATIONS

Protected left-turn phasing can help reduce the overall risk of pedestrian injury and decreases the potential for crashes.

Use of protected phasing may increase the overall signal cycle length, reducing the overall time available for pedestrian crossings and increasing wait times for all movements.

While protected left turn phasing bears consideration in certain locations, a city may elect to restrict left turns entirely or for specific portions of the day when risk of collision is most acute.

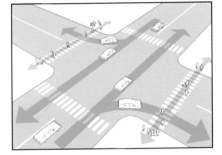

LEFT TURN RESTRICTIONS

Restricting left turns eliminates the conflict between left turns, oncoming motorist and bicyclist through traffic, and pedestrians. These restrictions may shift the conflict to a more desirable location along the corridor and have been successfully implemented by time of day in many cities.

APPLICATION

Eliminating left turns at an intersection is most often applied in the following situations:

- Intersections in a grid network of streets with adjacent intersections better able to handle additional phases in the signalized intersection (depending on block length);
- at locations where pedestrians or cyclists may experience risk associated with left turning traffic;
- and intersections where crossing traffic is significantly high and person carrying capacity may be a higher priority than local automobile accessibility.

BENEFITS & CONSIDERATIONS

Left turn restrictions can help reduce the overall risk of pedestrian injury and decrease

Eliminating a left turn movement at a particular location reduces the total lost time for the intersection, thus increasing the person carrying capacity of the intersection and reducing the overall cycle length.

Left turn restrictions reduce the conflict between through moving traffic and left turns, improving overall safety at the intersections.

Restrictions can be managed by time of day, though time of day restrictions may require additional enforcement and adequate signage to ensure comprehension.

Signal Cycle Lengths

Corridor-Based Signal Timing with Longer Cycles

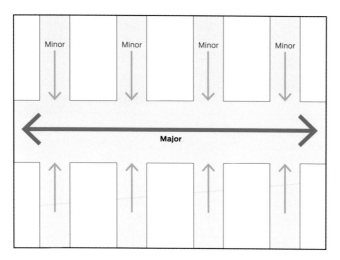

Corridor-based cycle lengths (sec)

Longer signal cycles and corridor-based timing schemes make large avenues into barriers that separate neighborhoods rather than join them.

Under the initial conditions shown above, all users approaching from side streets incur significant delay when crossing the major corridor. The major corridor receives almost four times as much green time (96 seconds) as the minor streets (24 seconds). As a result, motorists avoid minor streets, increasing congestion on main routes. Pedestrians frequently cross the street out of frustration before receiving a WALK signal.

Balanced Signal Timing with Shorter Cycles

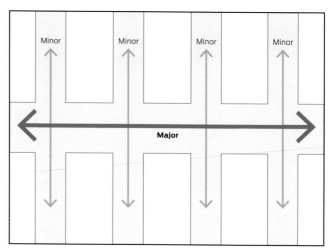

Balanced cycle lengths (sec)

Shorter signal cycles help city streets function as a complete network, rather than a series of major corridors.

In the balanced scenario, the signals are retimed with 60-second cycle lengths. The amount of green time at each minor intersection is apportioned in a 3:2 ratio (36 seconds for the major street, 24 for the minor). The increased turnover improves pedestrian compliance and decreases congestion on surrounding streets.

DISCUSSION

Though often invisible to the public, traffic signal cycle lengths have a significant impact on the quality of the urban realm and, consequently, the opportunities for bicyclists, pedestrians, and transit vehicles to operate safely along a corridor. Long signal cycles, compounded over multiple intersections, can make crossing a street or walking even a short distance prohibitive and frustrating. This discourages walking altogether, and makes streets into barriers that separate destinations, rather than arteries that stitch them together.

BENEFITS & CONSIDERATIONS

Short signal cycles reduce overall pedestrian wait times as well as side street delay.

Shortening cycle lengths can come at the expense of reducing the amount of time that a pedestrian has to cross the street. While long cycle lengths may increase pedestrian non-compliance and risk-taking behavior, short cycle lengths may not always be achieved without resorting to a 2-stage pedestrian crossing, especially on wider streets and boulevards. Determination of the appropriate cycle length must always be correlated with the pedestrian crossing distance on a given street.[2]

Cycle lengths influence the desired progression speed of traffic along a corridor. They may be used to keep speeds to a minimum as part of a coordinated signal timing plan. Longer cycle lengths result in wider variability in speeds.

CRITICAL

A minimum WALK time of 7 seconds is required (MUTCD 4E.06). WALK times should be dictated by the overall crossing distance and based on a minimum crossing speed of 2.5–3.5 feet per second.

RECOMMENDED

Short cycle lengths of 60–90 seconds are ideal for urban areas and permit frequent gaps and consistent crossing opportunities, creating a more permeable network.

The length of a pedestrian crossing should be taken into account when using shorter cycle lengths. In some cases, elderly pedestrians and children may be unable to cross in a single cycle. In these cases, efforts must be made to shorten the crossing via road diets, curb extensions, and other measures.

While short cycle lengths are desirable, ensure that cycle lengths are long enough for pedestrians to cross wide streets in a single leg without getting stuck in the median, unless the median is a destination in and of itself.

Adaptive signal control should have limited variation in their cycle length. Operations for adaptive signal control should be limited to suburban settings and event venues where traffic is highly

LOS ANGELES, CA
High visibility crosswalks have few benefits if the average pedestrian is not given sufficient time to cross the street or delayed considerably.

variable. Adaptive signal control can result in a longer cycle length that degrades multi-modal conditions.

OPTIONAL

Cycle lengths may be adjusted according to the time of day to account for fluctuating vehicle or pedestrian volumes. Cycle length adjustments should be minimal and consider both pedestrian and vehicle volumes at peak and off-peak times.

Cycle lengths shorter than 60 seconds are only recommended where a city uses "feathering" (intervals that decrease as they approach a pinch point) to relieve an upstream bottleneck. In such cases, adequate crossing time for pedestrians should be taken into account based on a crossing speed between 2.5–3.5 feet per second.[3]

Fixed vs. Actuated Signalization

APPLICATION

In general, fixed-time signals are the rule in urban areas for reasons of regularity, network organization, predictability, and reducing unnecessary delay.

In certain, less-trafficked areas, actuated signals (push buttons, loop detectors) may be appropriate; however, these must be programmed to minimize delay, which will increase compliance. Actuated signals, in general, are not preferable because of the maintenance requirements and upkeep of the detection on the street.

BENEFITS & CONSIDERATIONS

Drivers and others at downstream unsignalized intersections benefit from a series of fixed-time signals, as they produce routine gaps in traffic that may be used to turn onto or cross the street. Fixed-time signals help make pedestrians an equal part of the traffic signal system by providing them with regular and consistent intervals at which to cross.

Fixed-time signals incur lower initial and ongoing maintenance costs than actuated signals.

Actuated signals prioritize movement along the primary corridor and can present obstacles to cross traffic and pedestrians if timed to prioritize vehicle movements only.

Where used, actuated signals should be timed to be as responsive to activation as possible, with delay kept to a minimum.

Many existing traffic signal controllers have the capacity to reduce delay, but remain in coordination rather than a free setting. Coordination, paired with long signal cycles, can result in delays of 80 seconds or more, reducing pedestrian compliance, increasing risk-taking behavior, and creating the impression that a push button is either non-responsive or malfunctioning.

At crossings where the signal is uncoordinated with adjacent traffic signals (free setting), designers can further reduce pedestrian delay by reducing the minimum green time. At coordinated signal locations, designers have multiple options to decrease delay, including increasing the permissive window, adjusting signal timing for responsiveness at certain times of day, and setting the signal to recall on the pedestrian phase.

CRITICAL

In coordination with traffic signal timing, designers must consider spacing between traffic signals, looking at desirable crossing intervals to achieve a pedestrian-friendly environment.

RECOMMENDED

Fixed-time signals are recommended in all downtown areas, central business districts, and urban areas in which pedestrians are anticipated or desired and speeds are intended to be low.

Use of semi- or fully actuated signal operations should mainly be restricted to suburban arterials and rural roads. In suburban corridors, motorist compliance can be increased and delay reduced through use of actuation.

In areas with lower pedestrian traffic, actuation may be used along priority rapid transit corridors to increase the schedule reliability of transit service and avoid unnecessary delays.

In areas with lower pedestrian traffic, actuation may be used along priority rapid transit corridors to increase the schedule reliability of transit service and avoid unnecessary delays.

The responsiveness of an actuated signal should be prompt (as low as 5 seconds) based on the necessary transition time for approaching motorists to come safely to a stop. In cases where the pedestrian movement crosses a high-capacity transit line, major bicycle facility, or critical freight route, longer delays are acceptable

For major bicycle routes, use upstream passive detection as opposed to push-button activation to minimize the time lag between detection and crossing.

OPTIONAL

Fully actuated signal control may be used where vehicle and pedestrian volumes vary considerably throughout the day. Full actuation can reduce the amount of delay by being responsive to ongoing shifts and patterns in the traffic system.

Semi-actuated control prioritizes the through movement of a major road and is not recommended on streets with frequent cross traffic or pedestrian demand from the minor approach unless a low cycle length is used (below 80 seconds). Any traffic signal with long delays for pedestrians may discourage crossings and become a barrier to travel, especially at busy intersections.

Actuated signals may be combined with a number of signalization treatments, including full signalization (of the major and minor approach) and pedestrian or half signalization (stop sign on the minor approach).

Signalization is not always the best option for a given intersection. Stop or yield control may be preferable at intersecting local or residential streets.

Coordinated Signal Timing

APPLICATION

Coordinated signal timing synchronizes traffic movements and manages the progression speed of specific modes where uninterrupted flow is desired along a corridor. While traditionally applied to increase vehicular traffic flow and reduce peak-hour delay, coordinated signal timing can also be optimized for slower speeds, creating an uninterrupted flow for bicyclists or low vehicle progression speeds for a pedestrian-friendly downtown. Signals may also be timed to coordinate transit headways along routes where regular transit service is consistent and has low variability.

Coordinated signal timing is typically applied on corridors with closely spaced intersections (1/4 mile or less), and where there is evidence of a desire for "platooning"—the seamless flow of a given street user or set progression speed. Where applied, coordinated signal timing should meet the specific goals and parameters of the surrounding context.

BENEFITS & CONSIDERATIONS

Coordination of traffic signals can reduce the number of stops along a corridor and provide for a continuous flow of traffic at the target speed. Progression speeds should be set at or below the target speed, rather than existing 85th-percentile speeds.

Care should be taken to develop off-peak signal timing plans that respect the lower-traffic conditions that may benefit from a much lower cycle length than the peak hour. Similarly, weekend signal timing plans should be responsive to the needs of the community.

SIGNAL TIMING CATEGORIZATION

Cycling Streets
Bicyclists traveling at 12–15 mph receive a green indication at successive intersections, resulting in a platoon of bicyclists along a corridor.

Downtown Areas
Coordinated signal timing for downtown areas may be established where consistent pedestrian or bicycle travel has been prioritized over vehicle travel. In such cases, a designer may coordinate signals to reward slower driving speeds of 15–20 mph through the downtown area.

Coordination with Transit
On transit routes, shorter signal cycle lengths may improve transit times by increasing turnover and reducing side-street delay. Cycle lengths of 60 seconds are recommended for most transit routes without transit signal prioritization in effect. Intersections with transit signal priority may benefit from slightly longer cycle lengths due to the flexibility it provides an engineer to modify time on a cycle-by-cycle basis.[4]

Design
Controls

At the outset of any redesign or reconstruction, designers set forth key criteria that govern the ensuing design of the street. These parameters, referred to here as "design controls," critically shape design decisions.

Design Controls

High-quality design for city streets and intersections relies on a keen understanding of the analytical processes and assumptions underlying those technical decisions that shape streets. Design controls, from peak-hour traffic demand to level of service, should always be driven by the intended outcome of a design and the specific set of issues a project strives to resolve.

PASSIVE VS. PROACTIVE DESIGN

A passive design approach assumes, and strives to account for, the worst case scenario, both in terms of user behavior and traffic congestion. For many years, roadways have been designed with a "passive" approach, allowing drivers to travel unpredictably at high speeds. While a passive approach to system design is sound in parallel fields of engineering, such as stormwater management or seismic engineering for earthquake zones, its conse-quences for ordinary city streets have been disastrous. Overdesigned buffers, clear zones, and setbacks intended to account for fixed-object crashes have created streets that not only account for, but encourage, unsafe speeds.

Whereas storms and earthquakes are environmental factors whose impact can be tempered through design, human behavior, which governs traffic engineering, is fundamentally adaptable, not fixed. People adapt to their conditions. Changing streets change behavior, meaning that a street designed for the fastest and worst driver may very well create more drivers who feel comfortable at faster and more unsafe speeds. A proactive approach uses design to affect desired out-comes, guiding user behavior through physical and environmental cues.[1]

Design Speed

Speed plays a critical role in crashes and the severity of their outcomes. Traditional street design was grounded in highway design principles that forgive driver error and accommodate higher speeds. This approach based the design speed and posted speed limit on 85th-percentile speeds—how fast drivers are actually driving rather than how fast drivers ought to drive. By designing for a faster set of drivers, crashes increase and drivers actually traveling the speed limit are put at risk. This passive use of design speed accommodates, and indirectly encourages, speeding by designing streets that account for the worst set of drivers and highest potential risks. Higher design speeds, moreover, degrade city streets and walkable neighborhoods by mandating larger curb radii, wider travel lanes, guardrails, streets with no on-street parking, and generous clear zones.

Lowering injuries and fatalities remains a crucial goal for our cities. In 2011, 4,432 pedestrians were killed and 69,000 injured in motor vehicle crashes, according to the National Highway Traffic Safety Administration (NHTSA). Of the fatalities, 73% occurred in urban areas. This equates to 146 people killed or injured in cities everyday. To counteract these gruesome and unnecessary injuries and fatalities, cities should utilize speed control mechanisms that influence behavior, lower speeds, and in turn, reduce injuries and fatalities. Embracing a proactive design approach on new and existing streets with the goal of reducing speeds "may be the single most consequential intervention in reducing pedestrian injury and fatality."[1]

DISCUSSION

Speed plays a critical role in the cause and severity of crashes. There is a direct correlation between higher speeds, crash risk, and the severity of injuries.[3]

On city streets, designers should select a design speed to use in geometric decisions based on safe operating speeds in a complex environment.

10–15 MPH

Driver's peripheral vision

Stopping distance

Crash risk

20–25 MPH

Driver's peripheral vision

Stopping distance

Crash risk

30–35 MPH

Driver's peripheral vision

Stopping distance

Crash risk

40+ MPH

Driver's peripheral vision

Stopping distance

Crash risk

As a driver's speed increases, his peripheral vision narrows severely.[2]

Higher speeds =
Higher crash risk =
Higher injury severity =
Lower safety

SPEED (MPH)	STOPPING DISTANCE (FT)*	CRASH RISK (%)†	FATALITY RISK (%)†
10–15	25	5	2
20–25	40	15	5
30–35	75	55	45
40+	118	90	85

* Stopping Distance includes perception, reaction, and braking times.

† Source: Traditional Neighborhood Development: Street Design Guidelines (1999), ITE Transportation Planning Council Committee 5P-8.

Higher design speeds often mandate larger curb radii, wider travel lane widths, on-street parking restrictions, guardrails, and clear zones. Lower design speeds reduce observed speeding behavior, providing a safer place for people to walk, park, and drive.

CONVENTIONAL HIGHWAY DESIGN:

Operating Speed = Design Speed = Posted Speed

PROACTIVE URBAN STREET DESIGN:

Target Speed = Design Speed = Posted Speed

MASS DIFFERENTIAL

Mass differential between street users results in more severe injuries to the lighter of the two colliding bodies.

Bus
24,000 lbs

Car
2,000 lbs

Cyclist/ Pedestrian
30–250 lbs

CRITICAL

Design streets using target speed, the speed you intend for drivers to go, rather than operating speed. The 85th percentile of observed target speeds should fall between 10–30 mph on most urban streets.

The maximum target speed for urban arterial streets is 35 mph.[4] Some urban arterials may fall outside of built-up areas where people are likely or permitted to walk or bicycle. In these highway-like conditions, a higher target speed may be appropriate.

The maximum target speed for urban collector or local streets is 30 mph.

Use design criteria that are at or below the target speed of a given street. The use of higher speeds should be reserved for limited access freeways and highways and is inappropriate on urban streets, including urban arterials.

Bring the design speed in line with the target speed by implementing measures to reduce and stabilize operating speeds as appropriate. Narrower lane widths, roadside landscaping, speed humps, and curb extensions reduce traffic speeds and improve the quality of the bicycle and pedestrian realm.[5]

RECOMMENDED

Use short cycle lengths and/or slow signal progressions in downtown areas and networks with closely spaced signals.

In neighborhoods, designers should consider 20 mph zones to reduce speeds to those safe for interaction with children at play and other unpredictable behavior.

On local roads or in areas with above-average pedestrian volumes, designers may choose to select a design speed below the posted speed limit. Certain states disallow posted speeds of less than 25 mph, but do not restrict operating speeds 10 mph below the speed limit.

OPTIONAL

Shared streets and alleys may be assigned target speeds as low as 5–10 mph.

Speed enforcement cameras have proven highly effective at reducing speeds and increasing compliance with the speed limit.

NEW ORLEANS, LA
Narrow streets lower traffic speeds.

CHICAGO, IL
A mini roundabout slows speeds through a residential area.

Speed Reduction Mechanisms

Cities can achieve a reduction in traffic speeds using a variety of traffic calming techniques. While certain speed controls alter the configuration of a roadway, others change how people psychologically perceive and respond to a street. Consider the following tools to encourage motorists to drive at target speeds.

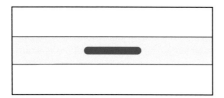

Median
Medians create a pinchpoint for traffic in the center of the roadway and can reduce pedestrian crossing distances.

Pinchpoint
Chokers or pinchpoints restrict motorists from operating at high speeds on local streets and significantly expand the sidewalk realm for pedestrians.

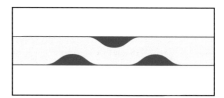

Chicane
Chicanes slow drivers by alternating parking or curb extensions along the corridor.

Lane Shift
A lane shift horizontally deflects a vehicle and may be designed with striping, curb extensions, or parking.

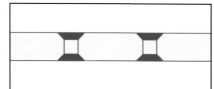

Speed Hump
Speed humps vertically deflect vehicles and may be combined with a midblock crosswalk.

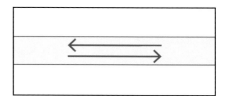

2-Way Street
2-way streets, especially those with narrower profiles, encourage motorists to be more cautious and wary of oncoming traffic.

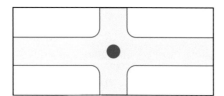

Roundabout
Roundabouts reduce traffic speeds at intersections by requiring motorists to move with caution through conflict points.

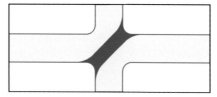

Diverter
A traffic diverter breaks up the street grid while maintaining permeability for pedestrians and bicyclists.

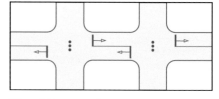

Signal Progression
Signals timed to a street's target speed can create lower speeds along a corridor.

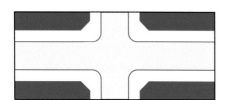

Building Lines
A dense built environment with no significant setbacks constrains sightlines, making drivers more alert and aware of their surroundings.

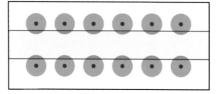

Street Trees
Trees narrow a driver's visual field and create rhythm along the street.

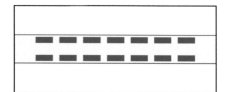

On-Street Parking
On-street parking narrows the street and slows traffic by creating friction for moving vehicles.

Design Vehicle

Design for the most vulnerable street user rather than the largest possible vehicle. While designs must account for the challenges that larger vehicles, especially emergency vehicles, may face, these infrequent challenges must not dominate the safety or comfort of a site for the majority of daily users. The selection of design vehicle influences the physical characteristics, safety, and operations of a roadway.

DISCUSSION

The selection of a design vehicle impacts the ultimate design characteristics of that street.[1] Before selecting a design vehicle, consider the ideal design given the overall context of the roadway, understanding how larger vehicles might flexibly operate within the proposed design.[2]

Curb radii designed to accommodate the largest possible vehicle at its highest possible speed degrade the pedestrian environment and result in longer crossing distances.[3]

Large emergency vehicles, such as fire trucks, have certain ideal dimensions for operation often tied to response times. Assume that emergency vehicles are permitted full use of the right-of-way in both directions, especially where tight curb radii may necessitate use of the opposite lane during a turn.[4]

Transit vehicles, such as articulated buses, benefit from the use of a larger effective turning radius, which is benefitted by bikeways and/or on-street parking.

Oversized trucks and other large vehicles may be restricted from certain corridors based on existing context, vulnerable street users, or impractical operational impacts. Reroute trucks to parallel routes where extensive reconstruction is not required to meet their needs.

CRITICAL

The design vehicle is a frequent user of a given street and dictates the minimum required turning radius; a control vehicle is an infrequent large user. The design vehicle can turn using one incoming and one receiving lane; the control vehicle can turn using multiple lane spaces.

Large trucks infrequently require access to local streets. These vehicles may use opposite lanes to complete the turn.

Adopt both a design vehicle and a control vehicle standard based on context-specific city street types. The design vehicle determines the design of elements such as turning radius and lane width. The control vehicle dictates how the design might accommodate a larger vehicle's turning needs when using the whole intersection.[5]

City transit buses must be able to turn on bus routes without resorting to a 3-point operation. Where a 3-point turn would be necessary, designers should consider removing parking spaces near the intersection or recessing the stop line on the receiving street.

BROOKLYN, NY

At this intersection, a frequent bus route requires a tight right turn. A recessed stop line paired with a "stop here" sign is used so the bus can complete its turn in one maneuver.

Controlling Turn Speeds and Recessed Stop Bars

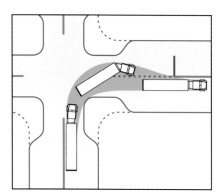

Allowing infrequent vehicles to use the whole intersection (moving left slightly before the turn and using the lane adjacent to the right lane on the receiving side) allows the entire intersection to become more compact, reducing turning speeds of regular vehicles to 12–15 mph. A recessed stop bar prevents conflicts with opposing traffic.

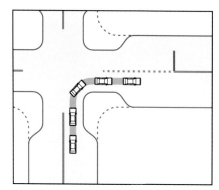

Using a smaller design vehicle but allowing for occasional larger vehicles to use the entire intersection allows the design to promote a typical turning speed of 5–10 mph.

Use "crawl" speeds, as opposed to design speed, when determining local street geometry factors associated with the design vehicle.[6] Vehicles traveling at slower speeds have more flexibility and can make difficult turns that may be challenging or unsafe at higher speeds.

A motor coach turns on a small residential neighborhood street at "crawl" speed.

RECOMMENDED

Adopt a new design vehicle that is a frequent user of urban streets—the delivery truck (DL-23). Package delivery trucks commonly travel on city streets, and have an inside turning radius of 22.5 feet and an outside turning radius of 29 feet.

CHICAGO, IL
This truck is an example of the DL-23.

All truck routes should be designed to permit the safe and effective operation of trucks. Designation of freight routes should be considered in coordination with mapping of primary bicycle, transit, and pedestrian corridors, as well as through the analysis of key access routes, bridge hazards, and industrial or commercial land uses. Pair truck route programming with enforcement to ensure that oversize vehicles are not diverting off-network.

The design vehicle types below should be considered in order to maintain property access while emphasizing pedestrian safety and low speeds.

STREET TYPE	DESIGN VEHICLE
Neighborhood and Residential Streets	DL-23 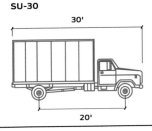
Downtown and Commercial Streets	SU-30 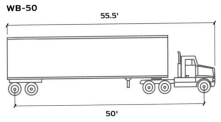
Designated Truck Routes Note: Trucks are permitted to use the full intersection when making turns onto a receiving street.	WB-50 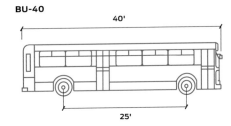
Designated Bus Routes Note: Buses are permitted to use the full intersection when making turns onto a receiving street, but this is not preferable on a full-time bus route if it can be avoided.	BU-40

The largest frequent user of urban streets is the DL-23.

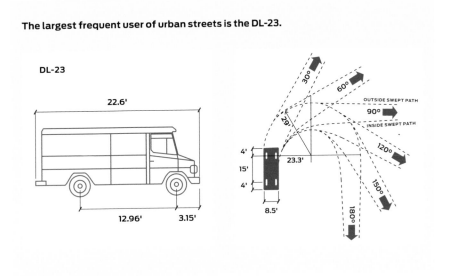

DL-23

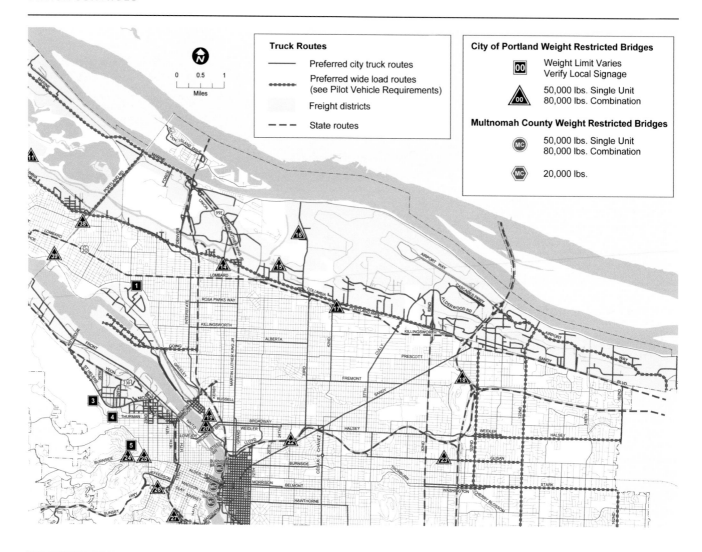

Truck Routes

— Preferred city truck routes

•••••• Preferred wide load routes
(see Pilot Vehicle Requirements)

Freight districts

– – – State routes

City of Portland Weight Restricted Bridges

00 Weight Limit Varies
Verify Local Signage

▲ 00 50,000 lbs. Single Unit
80,000 lbs. Combination

Multnomah County Weight Restricted Bridges

MC 50,000 lbs. Single Unit
80,000 lbs. Combination

MC 20,000 lbs.

Where truck routes intersect and frequent turns are made, install bollards at the intersection corner to help prevent injuries and fatalities from truck wheels overrunning the curb.[7]

///

OPTIONAL

On narrow commercial streets that require frequent loading and unloading, consider the application of a shared street design to avoid large turning radii or freight vehicles parking on sidewalks.

Portland's freight master plan *(above)* classified truck routes and created freight districts.[8]

Where trucks or city buses are expected to frequently encroach on the centerline, consider using a dashed centerline at the potential conflict point at the intersection.

Design Hour

A street's uses, demands, and activities are subject to change over the course of a day. A street at rush hour behaves differently than it does at lunch hour, just as a street late on a Saturday night is used differently on Sunday morning. Street design should be sensitive to how streets operate across all hours of the day, for all users. While understanding peak periods of intensity is valuable, the design of a street or analysis of a corridor should always seek to balance needs and functions of different time periods.

DISCUSSION

Vibrant cities are active 24 hours a day. Streets designed for peak intervals of traffic flow relieve rush-hour congestion, but may fail to provide a safe and attractive environment during other portions of the day. Average Daily Traffic (ADT) and peak volumes alone do not reveal a street's utilization. Instead, consider multiple hours of travel and average traffic per lane.

Travel time between similar origin and destination pairs tend to be similar across different routes within the network. When one route becomes congested, users choose a different route.[1]

Urban traffic networks and grids are flexible and resilient due to their inherent connectivity. Design streets from a network perspective, considering turn restrictions and 1-way to 2-way conversions, as well as the overall distribution of congestion throughout the network.

Consider the peak-time activities of pedestrians and bicycles as well as traffic. For pedestrians, peak hours often fall near lunchtime, while bicyclist peak hours typically follow a similar pattern to vehicle traffic, except in cases where demand for greenways or recreational centers peaks on weekends.

Peak congestion conditions are subject to adjustment, as drivers may change their behavior based on expected delay.

A DAY IN THE LIFE OF A STREET

8:00 am

AM PEAK
Signals are adjusted to accommodate rush-hour traffic during the peak hour, metering traffic to prevent gridlock.

1:00 pm

MID-DAY
Downtown pedestrian volumes reach their peak intensity at lunch hour.

8:00 pm

EVENING
Traffic volumes begin to dip in the evening, after rush hour, while pedestrian traffic in certain areas begins to rise.

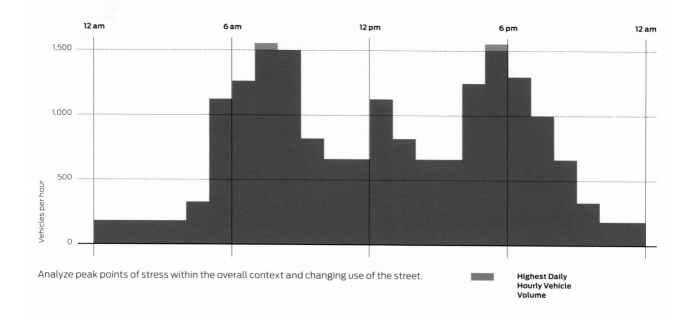

Analyze peak points of stress within the overall context and changing use of the street.

Highest Daily Hourly Vehicle Volume

Collect multi-modal data over 2–3 hours of peak traffic activity to better understand how traffic behaves through an entire rush-hour period.

RECOMMENDED

Residential areas should be designed to enhance the public realm during off-peak hours, while retail corridors may require sidewalk design parameters that accommodate pedestrian flows on weekends and holidays. Transit priority lanes and parking lanes may be governed flexibly throughout the day, with curbside bus lanes being converted to parking on weekends or dedicated loading zones at early morning hours.

Use signal timing or transportation demand management to shift congestion rather than relying upon capacity increases.

Collect 4-hour volumes (AM peak, midday, PM peak, and Saturday) to analyze typical traffic levels. Average these 4 hours and use that volume to guide the design of streets and intersections.[2]

Utilize performance measures that demonstrate overall corridor travel times as opposed to specific intersection peak level of service only.

Most cities apply ITE's *Trip Generation* standards to new developments. Ensure that generated trips are assigned to multiple modes based upon existing mode splits or city-adopted mode targets. This reduces additional peak hour vehicle trips generated by the development site and reduces required mitigations.[4]

42,000 ADT, Hour by Hour

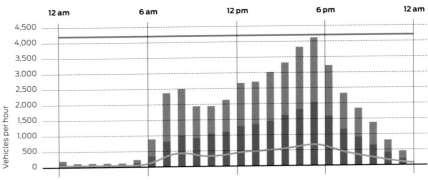

Broadway Boulevard at Kolb Road in Tucson, AZ is a 6-lane road. 24-hour traffic counts from 2012 illustrate conditions similar to many urban arterials in the country. ADT totals 42,207. Spread across a 24-hour period and accounting for average vehicles per lane, however, the amount of car traffic is well below capacity for nearly all hours of the day.[3]

▬	Westbound
▬	Eastbound
—	6-Lane Capacity (700 vpl)
—	Average Number of Vehicles per Lane (6 lanes)

Peak-hour parking restrictions for general purpose travel should be limited or converted to other uses. Peak-hour lanes in urban areas, especially those that are directly next to the pedestrian's path of travel, should be avoided. Peak-hour parking restrictions also limit the use of many other beneficial treatments, such as curb extensions, parklets, and bikeways.

WASHINGTON, D.C.
During peak hours, this 4-lane road becomes a 6-lane road, adding 50% more capacity but reducing opportunities for the 20 non-peak hours per day.

Peak-hour analysis has the potential to adversely impact streets in the following ways:

Intersection Design
Warrants for turning traffic often mandate the addition of left- and right-turn lanes to preserve high speeds for through traffic. Reallocate spacing for turn lanes within the existing right-of-way rather than widening the intersection.

Project and Development Review
Traffic impact analysis statements typically require a study of how to accommodate peak-hour volumes. Mitigate peak traffic using operational strategies rather than resorting to increased roadway capacity.

Level of Service (LOS) Calculations
Peak hour volumes are fed into calculation of LOS, which is used to justify costly capacity increases.[5]

Analyze streets for all users at both peak and off-peak times to understand their needs and uses within the system. Based on these analyses, explore reallocation and street management tactics, such as temporary pedestrian streets, to better take advantage of the rights-of-way over the course of a single day, week, or year.

OPTIONAL

Restrict parking in favor of high-activity loading zones during morning hours to avoid double-parking on major commercial streets.

Implement combined High-Occupancy Vehicle (HOV)/transit lanes on heavily traveled corridors where HOV traffic would not interfere with transit operations.

Network Solutions

To solve peak-hour congestion at one location, look for solutions at the network level. Restricting turns at some locations or removing turn restrictions elsewhere in the grid funnels traffic onto alternate, less-congested routes.

Turn Restriction

New Pattern

Design Year

Cities must make investments that consider the life and longevity of any major infrastructure investment, accounting for anticipated future growth and development. Such projections should reflect a city's adopted goals and project an intended outcome, coordinated with land use controls.

The design year assigned to a roadway represents an estimation of the future traffic demand and volume expected on that facility. Design year typically relies on travel demand models and other methods that often implicitly assume steady traffic growth. These projections tend to stand at odds with both local policy and recent travel trends. While travel demand modeling has evolved into a highly sophisticated and refined field, it still remains an educated estimate and should be qualified by intended outcomes and goal-driven city policies.

Vehicle Miles Traveled (VMT) Per Capita

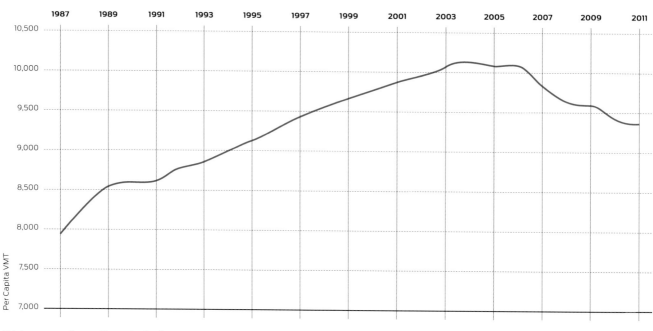

Driving per capita continues to decline, even as gas prices have stabilized and the economy has shown signs of recovery.
Source: State Smart Transporation Initiative (SSTI)[1]

——————— **Per Capita VMT**

While trends indicate that traffic volumes have leveled off or even decreased over the past 10 years in jurisdictions throughout the United States, traditional forecasting substantially overestimates the potential for traffic growth.[2] Similarly, many modeling efforts underestimate the potential bene-fits (traffic reduction impacts) of improved land use decisions, natural growth in other modes (such as bicycling) and an overall cultural shift in urban mobility choices.

A 2% compound traffic growth rate doubles traffic in 35 years.

TRAFFIC GROWTH PROJECTIONS

Federally funded projects and environ-mental reviews typically require the projection of traffic volumes 10–30 years in the future, typically assuming a 1–2% annual growth in vehicle volume.[3] These traffic projections are then analyzed in relation to existing performance measures (typically, level of service) to determine if future mitigations are necessary.

In most places, traffic projections are based on the selection of a transportation model (typically at the regional level), which is calibrated to emulate existing and future transportation levels based on land use, transportation investments, and other factors. A recent study investigated the post-construction accuracy of traffic forecasts and revealed that traffic on roads in urban settings (arterials and collectors) were typically overestimated by a significant amount.[4] Despite common logic, overdesigning and over-engineering a street from a roadway capacity standpoint may actually

be detrimental to public safety. Furthermore, overdesigning roadways to meet an inaccurate future demand presents a major opportunity cost for other land uses within a city's public realm.

City transportation policies often prioritize walking, bicycling, and transit. In some cases, cities aim to achieve explicit mode share targets to reduce dependence on single occupancy vehicle use.[5] Meeting these aggressive goals and targets will require a shift in both infrastructure investment and traveler behavior.

Individual projects should be assessed on a case-by-case basis to analyze how standard traffic growth factors (land-use trip generation, ambient growth) may conflict with or inhibit the desired diversification of street users and uses over time.[6] Future analysis should begin with the vision for future function of the street or facility, and identify design treatments (and in some cases policy) that will achieve this vision. In some cases, a negative VMT growth factor may be required to meet intended goals.

Traffic Evaporation

Retrofitting streets for pedestrians, cyclists, and transit may require reducing or reallocating roadway vehicle capacity. While prevailing perceptions equate reduced vehicular capacity with increased traffic congestion, research suggests the opposite. Referred to as "traffic evaporation," when road capacity is reduced (even in drastic amounts), vehicle volumes can actually respond by decreasing in similar proportion.[8] Based on numerous case studies, "reductions in road capacity have not been followed by prolonged gridlock, and major increases in existing levels of congestion are typically only temporary...Instead, there is a fairly substantial body of evidence to suggest that some proportion of traffic effectively 'disappears'..."[9, 10] Research suggests that the displaced traffic either (1) is absorbed by the surrounding street network, (2) shifts to another mode, or (3) the trip is altered (traveler changes destination or trip frequency).

Percent Change in Mode Share (2005–2011)

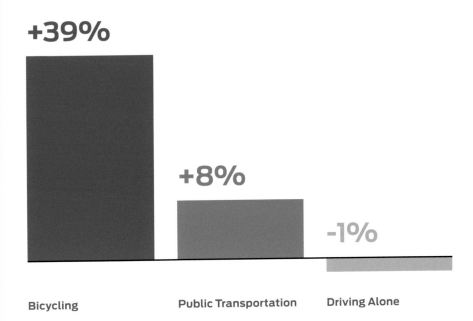

Mode share for public transportation and bicycling has increased dramatically over the past five years.
Source: USDOT Bureau of Transportation Statistics and the League of American Bicyclists[7]

Reflecting changing land uses and behaviors, projections may be utilized to satisfy warrants and other criteria for the installation of particular traffic control devices, such as stop signs, traffic signals, or other measures.

///

INDUCED DEMAND

The graphic at right illustrates how a road designed to a 20-year horizon induces traffic. The road is (re-) built with 20-year capacity, but is completed in 5 years. Drivers react to the additional road space by driving more, and expanded roadways built in recent years typically degrade the pedestrian experience, reducing the propensity of people to walk to schools, stores, or other destinations. Drivers also switch from alternative routes and earlier or later times for their commutes to fill the new capacity. The end result is that the road reaches its capacity in 10 years instead of 20.[11]

Induced Traffic Demand

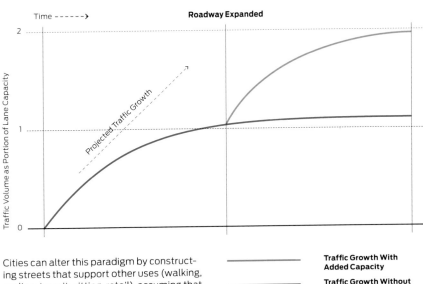

Cities can alter this paradigm by constructing streets that support other uses (walking, cycling, transit, sitting, retail), assuming that these choices will prompt more walking, cycling, and local retail activity.
Source: VTPI. "Smart Congestion Relief." 2013.

ALTERNATE METHODS

To supplement existing traffic models, several other strategies should be considered that may present more accurate estimates for future traffic demand.

Comparative Projection
While the *ITE Trip Generation Manual* is a frequently cited source, in urban settings the manual's outputs may not be a strong comparative match. To better meet the needs of urban settings, numerous research studies have been developed through universities and state DOTs that provide more precise trip generation rates for urban settings.[12]

Growth Projection
In many cities, traffic analysis requires the use of an "ambient growth factor," which reflects the underlying baseline traffic growth. This growth factor is often provided by city staff and is based on a moving average from past growth (typically 1–2%). This growth factor is often considered to be an assumed positive factor but should be strongly reconsidered due to its potential inaccuracies given recent cultural trends. Growth factors should no longer be strictly based on multiyear moving averages since recent VMT trends have been shown to be volatile (or declining). While growth projection factors of 1–2% seem minimal, it can have a significant cumulative impact over each year it is applied.

Mode Targets
Several U.S. cities (Chicago, Minneapolis, San Francisco, and others) and states have developed specific mode targets to achieve within a set time frame. For example, MassDOT has established a goal of tripling the number of trips by transit, bicycle, and walking. San Francisco has established a goal of 50% non-auto trips by 2018. These goals provide a set objective and spur the rapid implementation of programs that seek to accomplish them. These types of underlying programmatic shifts are often not explicitly integrated into traffic modeling efforts, but can serve as a baseline from which to better understand potential future modal shifts.

Greenhouse gas reductions
Another underlying factor that may play a major role in changing future traffic demand is greenhouse gas (GHG) emissions. Several states across the United States are employing GHG targets that filter down into several more tangible objectives (such as mode share, VMT reduction, and others). Massachusetts has established a target of 25% reduction in GHG by 2020 and 50% by 2050.[13]

Induced Demand Projection
If a project is determined to require an increase in roadway capacity, induced traffic demand should be considered a negative externality as a result. If the additional traffic demand created exceeds local policy thresholds (such as mode shift, as described above), it should be investigated if traffic can be mitigated through other non-roadway infrastructure strategies.

Performance Measures

Measuring the performance of a given street or network is a rigorous and imperfect process. A street that works extremely well for one set of users may be perilous for another, just as an intersection with no delay at one point may mask significant delay along a corridor. Performance measures must take a multidisciplinary approach, looking at urban streets and traffic at the macro and the micro scale, through the lens of safety, economy, and design, and inclusive of the goals and behaviors of everyone using the street.

The goals of different street users often stand at odds. Bicyclists come into conflict with unloading trucks, pedestrians vie with cars for crossing time at congested intersections, and emergency vehicle response times counter the desires of a community for slow traffic speeds and speed humps. Urban street design must strive to balance these goals, making strategic tradeoffs in search of a win-win scenario.

The development of holistic performance measures requires a redefinition of the problem that a designer is trying to solve, as well as recognition that streets are places to sit and stay as much as they are conduits for movement. While a multi-modal performance metric such as person delay may improve upon auto-based level of service (LOS), delay alone fails to capture the success of a city street outside of its ability to move people through it. A street with low "person delay" is not necessarily a great street, especially if it has no economic activity, places to sit and rest, or shade trees to improve the public realm.

PEDESTRIANS

1 People crave activity and variety at street level. Streets with active storefronts, foot traffic design, and human-scale design contribute toward an active and economically vibrant community. While activity is of paramount importance to the pedestrian realm, public safety, sidewalk width adequately spaced and apportioned, protection from rain, and shade from the sun together make the difference between a successful street and a barren one.

BICYCLISTS

2 Bicycle facilities should be direct, safe, intuitive, and cohesive. Bicyclists desire a high degree of connectivity and a system that functions well for cyclists of all skill levels, with minimal detour or delay.

Bicyclists benefit from feeling safe and protected from moving traffic. Bikeways that create an effective division from traffic and are well coordinated with the signal timing and intersection design of the traffic network form the basis of a accessible bicycle network.

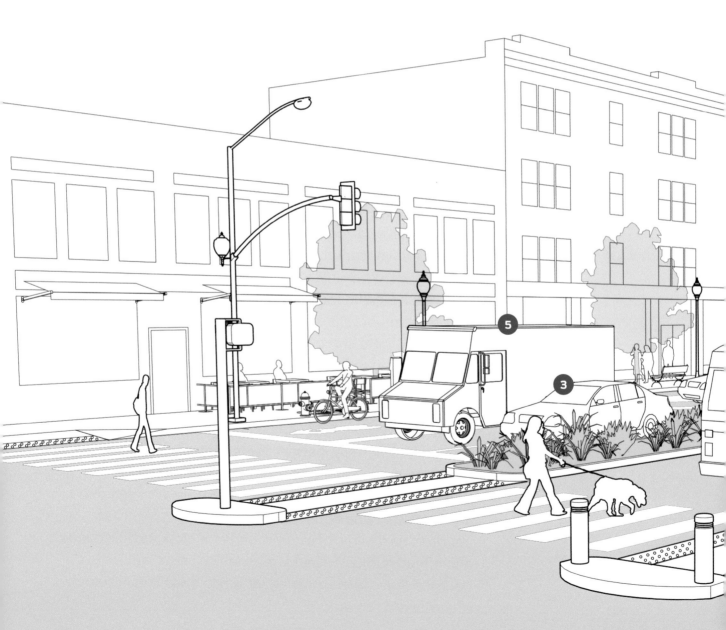

VEHICLES

3 Motorists want to get to their destination as quickly and safely as possible with limited friction, interruption, or delay. Vehicles typically benefit from limited-access, higher-speed roads with limited chance of conflict or surprise.

Due to their high speeds and overall mass, drivers feel safest when buffered from other moving vehicles, bicyclists, buses, trucks, and crossing pedestrians. Especially when making decisions at high speeds, motorists need adequate lighting and signage, as well as adequate parking provisions at their destinations.

TRANSIT

4 Transit service may be measured by its speed, convenience, reliability, and frequency of service. Trains and buses should permit easy loading and unloading, and be comfortable and not overcrowded. The overall level of access and scope of a transit network should be aligned to actual demand, meeting service needs without sacrificing service quality.

FREIGHT

5 Freight operators want to move goods from their origin to their destination as easily, quickly, and conveniently as possible. Trucks benefit from high—but not unsafe—speeds, curb access or docks for easy loading and unloading, and overall safety throughout the traffic system.

EMERGENCY VEHICLES

Emergency responders are responsible for attending to crimes, crashes, fires, and other dire scenarios as quickly as possible. They benefit from safety and predictability along their routes, with minimal conflicts with vehicles, bicyclists, or pedestrians, and direct curb access at their destinations.

LEVEL OF SERVICE

Level of service (LOS) measures the delay experienced by motorists at an intersection (or a specific lane at an intersection) according to a scale of A (least delay) through F (most delay). LOS is used to communicate the potential impact a new development or street reconfiguration may have at a particular intersection. Based on LOS data, a project can be assessed for the severity of anticipated congestion over a 20–30 year timeframe of the development.

LOS measures impacts, but inadequately captures a project's potential benefits. As a metric, it is mono-modal, measuring streets not by their economic and social vibrancy, but by their ability to process motor vehicles.

LOS is one of many tools that may be employed to assess traffic conditions in cities, but it should never be the only tool used. Cities should strive to integrate varied and holistic performance measures into their development review process, including measures that frame potential benefits, as well as those that capture risk.

ALTERNATE PERFORMANCE MEASURES

Cities are encouraged to use and adopt a variety of tools to complement or replace LOS as a performance measure. Below are some of the tools that cities are already using to assess conditions on their streets.

Pedestrians

· Safety: Rate of crashes, injuries, and fatalities (typically based on police records)
· Pedestrian LOS (Highway Capacity Manual)
· Public Life Surveys
· WalkScore (walkability ratings)
· Pedestrian Environmental Quality Index (PEQI)
· Minimal delay at crossings
· Foot-traffic volume

Bicyclists

· Safety: Crash records, injuries, and fatalities
· Bicycle LOS (Highway Capacity Manual)
· Travel Time and Delay
· Bicycle Environmental Quality index
· Bicycle counts

Vehicles

· LOS
· Travel Time
· Corridor Impact Analysis
· Safety: Crash records, injuries, and fatalities

Transit

· On-time performance
· Average speed
· Farebox recovery ratio
· Ridership per revenue hour
· Operating cost per hour

Freight

· Freight delivered by hour
· Time spent loading/unloading

Emergency Vehicles

· Response time

Sustainability

· LEED Neighborhood Development
· STARS
· GreenRoads

Multi-Modal

· Multi-Modal LOS
· Retail revenues and business growth

For a list of performance measures, see References, p. 174.

Level of Service: A

Level of Service: F

CASE STUDIES

Many communities have chosen to realign their performance measures with broader aims, including economic growth, public health, sustainability, and mode shift.

Washington, D.C.: Adopt Comprehensive Performance Measures

As both a project evaluation and benchmarking tool, performance measures beyond LOS are a centerpiece of the District's Great Streets program. The city tracks revitalization on under-invested corridors based on five main goals: economic health, safe and multi-modal transportation, community building, historical assets, and sustainable design.[1]

Chicago: Reduce Reliance on LOS

Chicago's Complete Streets Manual (2013) moves away from the LOS paradigm. The manual recommends using no minimum vehicle LOS and prioritizes pedestrian LOS, requiring no pedestrian delays in excess of 60 seconds.[2]

San Francisco: Phase Out LOS

San Francisco adopted its Transportation Sustainability Program in 2002. This policy mandates the gradual elimination of LOS, streamlines the project development review process, and replaces the Transportation Development Impact Fee levied against developers with the Transportation Sustainability Fee (TSF). The TSF offsets or reduces auto trips generated by a project with a fee used to support transit, pedestrian, and bicycle projects.[3]

Functional Classification

Functional classification is an ordering system that defines "the part that any particular road or street should play in serving the flow of trips through a highway network." Functional classification categorizes streets according to their ability to 1) move traffic and 2) provide access to adjacent properties. Street types under functional classification include "local streets," medium-sized "collectors," and highway-type "arterials."

Many city streets predated the advent of the Federal Highway System of functional classification, making the system unsuitable for the diversity of land uses and travel characteristics throughout an urban area. While certain types of classification make streets eligible for highway aid, once a street is given a class, federal design standards that do not consider local context may be assigned to that street, and any variation requires a design exception.

DISCUSSION

City streets are complex places where functional classification schemes— whether from a state agency or from the Federal Highway Administration— are generally too limiting as a basis for design capable of achieving social and economic goals for quality of life, mobility, and urban vitality. Such state or federal standards must be adapted to the urban environment before adoption so that city leaders maintain their flexibility to make streets a supportive element of a socially and economically thriving public realm.

Many cities use some form of street classification to provide stakeholders and developers with a set of standard street cross-sections to guide new development and rehabilitation. These set requirements for the construction of the street as well as dimensions for sidewalks, curbs, and setbacks. Federally defined functional classes, which are generally applied to National Highway System streets, have associated design guidelines used by some cities as well.

Even when they are completely updated, classification schemes, in and of themselves, are rarely adequate as a design tool for the diversity of situations to be encountered on city streets. Each project should also be approached with sound case-by-case professional judgment. In certain cases, cities may choose to alter a street's classification level to better align with a community's vision for its future.

Updated street design standards should be consistent with citywide goals for safety, economic growth, development, and urban design. These standards should attempt to capture the unique local relationship between the built realm and the surrounding streetscape, encapsulating the varying scales at which motorists, bicyclists, and pedestrians interact with individual corridors as well as the overall street network. This entails requiring sidewalks on urban arterials, enhancing the quality of street construction for special districts, and controlling access points to the property to reduce conflicts between driveway traffic and pedestrians.

Classification schemes, in and of themselves, are rarely adequate as a design tool for the diversity of situations to be encountered on city streets.

Many cities have developed street classification systems specific to their local needs. These classification systems generally combine 2–3 variables that guide decision making:

· Street type and usage

· Urban design context and built environment

· Overlays, including modal priorities, special uses, and historic designations

STREET	CONTEXT	OVERLAY
Avenue	Commercial	Country Route
Boulevard	Industrial	State Route
Street	Residential	
Arterial	City	Sanitation Route
Collector	Town	Snow Route
Local	Village	Truck Route
Alley	Campus	Ceremonial
Lane	Cultural	Economic
Main	Institutional	Historic
		Scenic
Connector	Center	Bicycle Priority
Major	Corridor	Driving Priority
Multi-Way	District	Pedestrian Priority
Thoroughfare	Downtown	Transit Priority
Transit		
Auto-Oriented	Low-Density	Home Zone
General	Marketplace	Pedestrian District
Multi-modal	Mixed-Use	Transit-Oriented
Parkway	Neighborhood	
Paseo	Park	
Pedestrian	Urban	
Shared	Workplace	
Slow		

SAN FRANCISCO'S BETTER STREETS PLAN

In December 2010, San Francisco's Board of Supervisors adopted a new, comprehensive street design guidebook, including developer requirements, entitled the *Better Streets Plan*. Numerous city codes were changed to facilitate implementation of the adopted guidelines on city streets. Any changes to the right-of-way must follow the new standards. These include necessary sidewalk-width, street trees, and intersection-design templates. The design guidance all corresponds to a series of street typologies that factor together street type and land use context.

San Francisco Streets Typology

· Parkways
· Park Edge
· Boulevards
· Ceremonial (Civic Streets)
· Commercial Throughways
· Downtown Commercial
· Downtown Residential
· Neighborhood Commercial
· Residential Throughway
· Mixed Use
· Industrial
· Shared Public Ways
· Paseo
· Alleys

Resources

Notes

Streets
For additional resources on streets, see References, p. 182.

STREET DESIGN PRINCIPLES

1   Richard Campbell and Margaret Wittgens, "The Business Case for Active Transportation: The Economic Benefits of Walking and Cycling," (Gloucester, ON: Go For Green, 2004).

Kelly Clifton, Christopher Muhs, Sara Morrissey, Tomás Morrissey, Kristina Currans, and Chloe Ritter, "Consumer Behavior and Travel Mode Choices," (Portland: Oregon Transportation Research and Education Consortium, 2012).

DOWNTOWN 2-WAY STREET

1   *Urban Freight Case Studies* (Washington, D.C.: USDOT, Federal Highway Administration Office of Freight Operations and Management, 2009)

"Loading and Delivery Management," *Better Market Street— Existing Conditions and Best Practices*, (San Francisco: City of San Francisco, 2011).

NEIGHBORHOOD MAIN STREET

1   *Evaluation of Lane Reduction 'Road Diet' Measures and Their Effects on Crashes and Injuries* (Washington, D.C.: Federal Highway Administration, Highway Safety Information System, 2010).

2   Nikiforos Stamatiadis and Adam Kirk, "Guidelines for Road Diet Conversions," (University of Kentucky, 2012).

3   Dan Burden and Peter Lagerwey, "Road Diets: Fixing the Big Roads," (Walkable Communities, Inc., 1999).

4   Cullen McCormick, "York Blvd: The Economics of a Road Diet," (2012).

NEIGHBORHOOD STREET

1   Raised crosswalks have been shown to increase motorists' yield rate by as much as 45%.

"Raised Pedestrian Crosswalks," *Safe Routes to Schools Guide* (Safe Routes to School, 2012).

YIELD STREET

1   For additional research on yield streets and skinny streets, see:

James M. Daisa and John B. Peers, "Narrow Residential Streets: Do They Really Slow Down Speeds," (Washington, D.C.: Institute for Transportation Engineers, 1987).

BOULEVARD

1   For further information about traffic control and operations on multiway boulevards, see:

Designing Walkable Urban Thoroughfares: A Context Sensitive Approach, (Washington, D.C.: Institute of Transportation Engineers, 2010), 82.

BOULEVARD

1   See "Bicycle Facility Evaluation," (District Department of Transportation, Washington, D.C.: 2012) for a case study of median bike lanes installed on Pennsylvania Avenue.

TRANSIT CORRIDOR

1   International cities with successful Bus Rapid Transit systems have played an instrumental role in shaping land use around transit corridors to ensure incentives for transit-oriented development.

Martha Panero, "Peer to Peer Information Exchange on Bus Rapid Transit (BRT) and Bus Priority Best Practices" (Washington, D.C.: Federal Transit Administration, 2012).

2   A.W. Agrawa, T. Goldman, and N. Hannaford, "Shared-Use Bus Priority Lanes on City Streets: Case Studies in Design and Management," Mineta Transportation Institute, Report 11–10 (2012).

"Designing Bus Rapid Transit Running Ways," (Washington, D.C.: American Public Transportation Association, 2010).

3   Shireen Chada and Robert Newland, "Effectiveness of Transit Signal Priority," National Center for Transit Research (2012).

Harriet Smith et al., "Transit Signal Priority: A Planning and Implementation Handbook," (Washington, D.C.: Federal Transit Administration, 2005).

GREEN ALLEY

1   Chicago's Green Alley Handbook provides guidance on alleyway design and suggestions for green alley adjacent properties.

The Chicago Green Alley Handbook, (Chicago: Chicago Department of Transportation, 2010).

Seattle's *Integrated Alley Handbook* estimates that the city contains 217,500 square feet of alleys, of which 85% are underused. This handbook provides excellent alley prototypes based on a variety of land uses. For more information, see:

Mary Fialko and Jennifer Hampton, *Seattle Integrated Alley Handbook: Activating Alleys for a Lively City*, (Seattle: University of Washington, 2011).

2 The City of Baltimore's Alley Gating and Greening Program enables neighbors adjacent to an alleyway to decide if they would like to partially or fully close the alleyway for greening projects.

   "Alley Gating & Greening Program," City of Baltimore, accessed May 31, 2013, http://www.baltimorecity.gov/ Government/AgenciesDepartments/GeneralServices/ AlleyGatingGreeningProgram.aspx.

3 The U.S. Environmental Protection Agency provides a wealth of literature related to green infrastructure, including bioswales, rain gardens, and other techniques for reducing the impact of large quantities of water during storms. For more information see the EPA's website on Green Infrastructure.

   "What is Green Infrastructure?," U.S. Environmental Protection Agency, accessed May 31, 2013, http://water.epa.gov/ infrastructure/greeninfrastructure/index.cfm.

   The City of Seattle's Street Edge Alternative Program's primary objective is to restore natural drainage patterns to manage stormwater and prevent flooding. The program achieves these objectives through the reduction of impervious surfaces and increases in planting and other natural elements.

   "Street Edge Alternatives," City of Seattle, accessed May 31, 2013, http://www.seattle.gov/util/environmentconservation/ projects/drainagesystem/greenstormwaterinfrastructure/ completedgsiprojects/streetedgealternatives/.

4 *Street and Site Plan Design Standards*, (Chicago: Department of Transportation, 2007), 23.

COMMERCIAL ALLEY

1 The San Francisco Better Streets Plan considers raised crosswalks at alleyways and shared public ways a standard treatment.

   San Francisco Better Streets Plan (San Francisco: City of San Francisco: 2012), 53

RESIDENTIAL SHARED STREET

1 Winthrop Street and Palmer Street in Cambridge, MA use benches and bollards to provide rough delineation along the traveled way portion of a shared street.

2 Warning strips enable a visually impaired individual to recognize that he or she is entering a space that may include vehicles.

   "Shared Use Path Accessibility Guidelines," *Federal Register Vol. 76, No. 59* (2011), 17069–17070.

3 Chicanes can be created through physical elements (street furniture, trees) or visual elements (pavers), but should not impede pedestrian travel through a shared street.

   San Francisco Better Streets Plan (San Francisco: City of San Francisco: 2012), 86.

COMMERCIAL SHARED STREET

1 The first pedestrian-only outdoor mall opened in Kalamazoo, MI, in 1959. For case studies of early pedestrian malls, see:

   Roberto Brambilla and Gianni Longo, *For Pedestrians Only: Planning, Design, and Management of Traffic-free Zones*, (New York: Whitney Library of Design, 1977).

2 The *San Francisco Better Streets Plan* provides guidance on "channels" and "runnels" that may be suitable for center street drainage.

   "Channels and Runnels," San Francisco Better Streets: A Guide to Making Street Improvements in San Francisco, accessed May 21, 2013, http://www.sfbetterstreets.org/ find-project-types/greening-and-stormwater-management/ stormwater-overview/channels-and-runnels/.

3 "Transit Mall Case Studies," (San Francisco County Transportation Authority).

Street Design Elements

LANE WIDTH

1 Theo Petrisch, "The Truth about Lane Widths," *The Pedestrian and Bicycle Information Center*, accessed April 12, 2013, http:// www.bicyclinginfo.org/library/details.cfm?id=4348.

2 Research suggests that lane widths less than 12 feet on urban and suburban arterials do not increase crash frequencies.

   Ingrid Potts, Douglas W. Harwood, and Karen R. Richard, "Relationship of Lane Width to Safety on Urban and Suburban Arterials," (paper presented at the TRB 86th Annual Meeting, Washington, D.C., January 21–25, 2007).

   Relationship Between Lane Width and Speed, (Washington, D.C.: Parsons Transportation Group, 2003), 1–6.

3 Eric Dumbaugh and Wenhao Li, "Designing for the Safety of Pedestrians, Cyclists, and Motorists in Urban Environments." *Journal of the American Planning Association* 77 (2011): 70.

   Previous research has shown various estimates of the relationship between lane width and travel speed. One account estimated that each additional foot of lane width related to a 2.9 mph increase in driver speed.

   Kay Fitzpatrick, Paul Carlson, Marcus Brewer, and Mark Wooldridge, "Design Factors That Affect Driver Speed on Suburban Arterials": *Transportation Research Record* 1751 (2000): 18–25.

Other references include:

Potts, Ingrid B., John F. Ringert, Douglas W. Harwood and Karin M. Bauer. *Operational and Safety Effects of Right-Turn Deceleration Lanes on Urban and Suburban Arterials.* Transportation Research Record: No 2023, 2007.

Macdonald, Elizabeth, Rebecca Sanders and Paul Supawanich. *The Effects of Transportation Corridors' Roadside Design Features on User Behavior and Safety, and Their Contributions to Health, Environmental Quality, and Community Economic Vitality: a Literature Review.* UCTC Research Paper No. 878. 2008.

4   Longer crossing distances not only pose as a pedestrian barrier but also require longer traffic signal cycle times, which may have an impact on general traffic circulation.

SIDEWALKS

1   A 2003 newsletter of "Let's Talk Business" cited several economic benefits of walkable communities, including a case study from Lodi, CA that cited how pedestrian improvements paired with economic development incentives dropped the retail vacancy rate from 18% to 6% and also resulted in a 30% increase in downtown sales tax revenues.

Bill Ryan, "Let's Talk Business: Ideas for Expanding Retails and Services in Your Community," *UW Extension*, July 2003.

A 2011 research study titled *Examining Walkability and Social Capital as Indicators of Quality of Life at the Municipal and Neighborhood Scales* used a case study approach between three communities in New Hampshire. Comparisons between the more walkable and less walkable neighborhoods show that levels of social capital are higher in more walkable neighborhoods.

Shannon H. Rogers, John M. Halstead, Kevin M. Gardner, and Cynthia H. Carlson, "Examining Walkability and Social Capital as Indicators of Quality of Life at the Municipal and Neighborhood Scales," *Applied Research Quality of Life* 6 (2010): 201–213.

2   Examples of higher standards for sidewalks include downtown Washington, D.C. (16 foot + 6 foot buffer), Chicago (varies between 10–12 feet depending on context), San Francisco (9–17 feet depending on context), Boston (target varies, but minimum is 7 feet for several street types).

3   As an example, Washington, D.C.'s *Design Engineering Manual* states that a sidewalk should exist on both sides of every street or roadway.

Design and Engineering Manual (Washington, D.C.: D.C. Department of Transportation, 2009): 29–3.

4   Joe Cortright, *Walking the Walk: How Walkability Raises Housing Values in U.S. Cities* (Chicago: CEOs for Cities, 2009).

5   Paul D. Thompson, Kevin M. Ford, Arman Mohammad, Samuel Labi, Arun Shirolé, and Kumares Siuha. *NCHRP Report 713: Estimating Life Expectancies of Highway Assets. Volume 1: Guidebook.* (Washington, D.C.: Transportation Research Board, 2012).

6   Federal Highway Administration, "Sidewalk Corridor Width," *Designing Sidewalks and Trails for Access* (Washington, D.C.: FHWA, 2001).

7   According to the American Disabilities Act, the minimum sidewalk width at bus stop loading points should be 8 feet to ensure clear boarding and alighting. The location of a bus shelter, bench, or other permanent fixtures should ensure a 3-foot clear path for pedestrian travel. However, 3 feet is not the recommended width for sidewalks, it is the absolute minimum needed to ensure a clear path of travel when obstacles exist in the sidewalk.

Americans With Disabilities Act of 1990.

8   "Where sidewalks are placed adjacent to the curb, the widths should be approximately 6 m [2 ft.] wider than the minimum required width. This additional width provides space for roadside hardware and snow storage outside the width needed by pedestrians."

A Policy on Geometric Design of Highways and Streets, 6th Edition (Washington, D.C.: AASHTO, 2011).

9   AASHTO's Roadside Design Guide defines a "clear zone as the total roadside border area, starting at the edge of the traveled way, available for safe use by errant vehicles. This area may consist of a shoulder, a recoverable slope, a non-recoverable slope, and/or a clear run-out area."

Roadside Design Guide, 4th Edition (Washington, D.C.: AASHTO, 2011).

10   In urban areas, the presence of fixed roadside objects (such as trees) is correlated with lower crash frequencies. This suggests that roadside objects in urban areas may actually enhance safety (by increasing driver caution and reducing speeds). As referenced in Eric Dumbaugh, "Safe Streets, Livable Streets," *Journal of the American Planning Association* 71 (2005): 295.

11   The AASHTO Green Book suggests a minimum offset distance of 1.5 feet between the face of the curb to the nearest fixed object off the roadway.

A Policy on Geometric Design of Highways and Streets, 6th Edition (Washington, D.C.: AASHTO, 2011).

CURB EXTENSIONS

1   Randal S. Johnson, *Pedestrian Safety Impacts of Curb Extensions: A Case Study* (Corvallis: Oregon State University, 2005).

2   Relocation can be costly. The city of San Francisco estimates the expense of relocating a fire hydrant at between $40,000–70,000. Allowing hydrants to remain in place offers cost savings. NYC DOT recommends curb extensions in front of hydrants to guarantee access where illegal parking is an issue, thereby benefiting emergency services.

Street Design Manual (New York: New York City Department of Transportation, 2009), 65.

San Francisco Better Streets Plan (San Francisco, 2010).

"Crossing Enhancements," Walking Info, accessed June 3, 2013, http://www.walkinginfo.org/engineering/crossings-enhancements.cfm.

"Traffic Calming Design Guidelines," New York City Department of Transportation, accessed June 3, 2013, http://www.nyc.gov/html/dot/html/pedestrians/traffic-calming.shtml.

3   In San Francisco, bus bays are being replaced with bus bulbs.
     Analysis shows that the bus bulbs increased vehicle and bus
     speeds between 7–46%. Experience in a variety of cities shows
     that bus bulbs combined with signal priority and automobile
     turn restrictions may significantly improve transit operating
     efficiency.

     Kay Fitzpatrick, Kevin M. Hall, Stephen Farnsworth, and Melisa
     D. Finley: *TCRP Report 65: Evaluation of Bus Bulbs* (Washington,
     D.C.: Transportation Research Board, 2001), 2.

4   Length and width of bus bulbs varies based on street geometry,
     vehicle types, and urban context. Thirty-foot bus bulbs are
     widely used for non-articulated buses operating two doors.
     Longer extensions may be required for articulated buses and
     shorter bulbs may be possible for buses operating a single door.
     In Portland, Oregon, all bus bulbs are 6 feet wide to provide a
     2-foot "shy zone" between the bulb and the travel lane.

     Kay Fitzpatrick et al., *TCRP Report 65: Evaluation of Bus Bulbs*
     (Washington, D.C.: Transportation Research Board, 2001), 5.

5   Cities adopt different interior radii based on street sweeping,
     snow removal, and design priorities. Wide, curving radii, where
     space allows, facilitate street cleaning. Sharper angles preserve
     more on-street parking. Forty-five-degree return angles allow
     for cleaning and preserve parking.

     San Francisco Better Streets Plan (San Francisco: City of
     San Francisco, 2010), 5.3.

     Best Practices for Pedestrian Master Planning and Design
     (Sacramento: Sacramento Transportation & Air Quality
     Collaborative, 2013), 14–15.

VERTICAL SPEED CONTROL ELEMENTS

1   For example, many speed hump programs prepare by clocking
     vehicle speeds and determining the 85th-percentile speeds in
     relation to the desired speed before installation takes place.

     *City of Redwood City Policy and Guidelines for Speed Hump
     Use* (Redwood: Redwood City Community Development
     Services, 1997).

2   NYC DOT takes applications for Slow Zones, projects that
     reduce the speed limit from 30 to 20 mph in residential areas,
     adding design and signage elements that enforce these lower
     speeds. Slow Zones typically measure 5 blocks by 5 blocks, or a
     quarter square mile.

     "Neighborhood Slow Zones," New York City Department of
     Transportation, accessed June 3, 2013,
     http://www.nyc.gov/html/dot/html/about/slowzones.shtml.

3   Portland installs 22-foot speed humps on streets with
     85th-percencile speeds of 35–45 mph.

     "Speed Bumps," *Bureau of Traffic Management Traffic Manual*
     (Portland: Portland Bureau of Transportation).

4   In one case study in King County, WA, the fire department found
     cushions minimized response time increases as compared to
     other traffic calming devices.

     Kevin Chang and Matthew Nolan, *An Evaluation of Speed
     Cushions on Neighborhood Streets: Balancing Emergency Vehicle
     Mobility With Traffic Calming Needs* (Washington, D.C.: Institute
     for Transportation Engineers, 2006).

TRANSIT STREETS

1   King County Metro is implementing bus-only lanes on a
     portion of Route 120, one of its top 10 busiest routes, with
     7,000 daily boardings.

     "Improving Route 120," Metro Transit, accessed May 30, 2013.
     http://metro.kingcounty.gov/have-a-say/projects/route120/.

     VTA in Vallejo, CA adopted service design guidelines with
     metrics such as boardings per revenue hour to transition local
     bus to BRT.

     Bus Rapid Transit Service Design Guidelines (San Jose: Santa
     Clara Valley Transportation Authority, 2007).

2   The New York City Department of Transportation, in partner-
     ship with New York City Transit (NYCT), the Metropolitan
     Transportation Authority, and City Council members, success-
     fully lobbied the state for legislation allowing installation of
     bus lane enforcement cameras as part of the new Select Bus
     Service (SBS), which has red-painted bus-only lanes. The SBS
     system uses two types of cameras. Fixed video cameras were
     installed on two routes beginning in November 2010. NYC DOT
     watches the footage and reports violations. Currently, NYCT
     is piloting cameras mounted on buses that take photos. Since
     SBS vehicles run on very short headways of 3–4 minutes,
     if a vehicle shows up on the two consecutive vehicles' cameras,
     a violation is recorded.

3   William Carry et al., "Red Bus Lane Treatment Evaluation,"
     Institute for Transportation Engineers (Washington, D.C.: 2012).

4   For additional information about ADA requirements at transit
     facilities, please see:

     "Bus Stops and Terminals," in *Accessibility Guidelines for
     Buildings and Facilities* (Washington, D.C.: Access Board: 1998).

5   For example, TriMet in Portland recommends shelters at stops
     with 50 or more weekday boardings.

     "Bus Stop Guidelines," (Portland: TriMet, 2012).

6   Michigan standards call for 115–230 feet between unsignalized
     intersections and driveways:

     "Standards for Access, Non-Motorized, and Transit," in
     Washtenaw County Access Management Plan (Ann Arbor:
     Michigan Department of Transportation 2008), 23.

STORMWATER MANAGEMENT

1   "Low Impact Development (LID)," U.S. Environmental
     Protection Agency, accessed June 3, 2013,
     http://water.epa.gov/polwaste/green.

     Noah Garrison and Karen Hobbs, *Rooftops to Rivers II: Green
     strategies for controlling stormwater and combined sewer
     overflows* (Washington, D.C.: National Resources Defense
     Council, 2011).

     "Managing Urban Runoff," U.S. Environmental Protection
     Agency, accessed June 3, 2013,
     http://water.epa.gov/polwaste/nps/urban.cfm.

2   "Chapter 3: Fundamentals of Stormwater Management,"
     New Hampshire Stormwater Manual (Concord: New Hampshire
     Department of Environmental Services, 2006).

3   "Deconstructing Green Infrastructure," Erosion Control,
     accessed June 3, 2013,
     http://www.erosioncontrol.com/EC/Articles/Deconstructing_
     Green_Infrastructure_17226.aspx.

4   "Why Green Infrastructure," U.S. Environmental Protection
     Agency, accessed June 3, 2013,
     http://water.epa.gov/infrastructure/greeninfrastructure/
     gi_why.cfm.

5   Jeffrey Odefey et al., *Banking On Green: A Look at How Green
     Infrastructure Can Save Municipalities Money and Provide
     Economic Benefits Community-wide* (American Rivers, Water
     Environment Federation, American Society of Landscape
     Architects, and ECONorthwest, 2012).

6   *Green City, Clean Waters: Green Infrastructure Maintenance
     Manual Development Process Plan* (Philadelphia: Philadelphia
     Water Department, 2012).

7   *Evaluation of Urban Soils: Suitability for Green Infrastructure
     or Urban Agriculture,* (Washington, D.C.: U.S. Environmental
     Protection Agency, 2011).

8   Nevue Ngan Associates et al. *Stormwater Management
     Handbook,* (Washington, D.C.: U.S. Environmental Protection
     Agency, 2009), Chapters 5–6.

9   "Permeable Pavement Systems," *Draft District of Columbia
     Stormwater Management Guidebook,* (Washington, D.C.:
     District Department of the Environment, 2012).

Interim Design Strategies

ACTIVATING THE CURB

1   Drew Meisel, *Bike Corrals: Local Business Impacts, Benefits, and
     Attitudes* (Portland: Portland State University, 2010).

PARKLETS

1   UCLA Luskin School of Public Affairs, *Reclaiming the Right of
     Way* (Los Angeles: University of California Los Angeles, 2012),
     148.

2   Parklet permit costs range from $1,000–2,000.

     San Francisco Parklet Manual (San Francisco: San Francisco
     Planning Department, 2013).

     Parklet FAQ (San Francisco: San Francisco Planning
     Department, 2013).

3   The Great Streets Project conducted a study in 2011 about the
     impacts of San Francisco parklets that found generally positive
     results relating to economics.

     Liza Pratt, *Parklet Impact Study* (San Francisco: SF Great
     Streets Project, 2011).

4   *Reclaiming the Right of Way* (Los Angeles: UCLA Luskin School
     of Public Affairs, University of California Los Angeles, 2012), 109.

5   For a comparison of various cities parklet standards, see:

     Reclaiming the Right of Way (Los Angeles: UCLA Luskin School
     of Public Affairs, University of California Los Angeles, 2012), 87.

6   *Philadelphia Parklet Program Guidelines* (Philadelphia: Mayor's
     Office of Transportation & Utilities, 2013).

TEMPORARY STREET CLOSURES

1   *Pedestrian & Transit Malls Study* (Memphis: Center City
     Commission, 2008).

     NYC DOT's report *Measuring the Street* found that
     various public space initiatives resulted in a 172% increase
     in retail sales.

     Measuring the Street: New Metrics for 21st Century Streets
     (New York: New York City Department of Transportation, 2012).

2   A *Journal of Urban Health* study examined the costs and
     health benefits of four Ciclovia events. The study found that
     benefits—in terms of economy and health—far outweigh the
     cost of the event. This is mostly because such events utilize
     existing infrastructure and are often the result of partnerships
     between public and private agencies.

     Felipe Montes et al., "Do Health Benefits Outweigh the Costs
     of Mass Recreational Programs? An Economic Analysis of
     Four Ciclovia Programs," *Journal of Urban Health: Bulletin of the
     New York City Academy of Medicine*, 89:1 (2011).

     Many health care providers have sponsored open street events.
     Blue Cross Blue Shield of Minnesota sponsored Open Streets
     events in 7 communities.

     Blue Cross and Blue Shield of Minnesota, "Blue Cross expands
     "Open Streets" events to seven Minnesota communities in 2012."

3   For a compendium of case studies on open streets
     programs, see:

     The Open Streets Guide (New York: Street Plans and Alliance
     for Biking & Walking, 2012).

INTERIM PUBLIC PLAZAS

1   *Measuring the Street: New Metrics for 21st Century Streets*
     (New York: New York City Department of Transportation, 2012).

2   *Street Design Manual,* (New York City: New York City
     Department of Transportation, 2009), Ch. 3.

3   The Madison Square public plaza in New York City is maintained by the Flatiron/23rd Street Partnership and the Madison Square Conservancy. Staff removes tables and chairs each night to prevent theft and clean the space.

Sabina Mollot, "Flatiron street to become pedestrian plaza," Flatiron 23rd Street Partnership, accessed June 3, 2013, http://www.flatironbid.org/documents/flatiron_triangles.pdf.

Intersection Design Elements

CORNER RADII

1   A literature review of the topic of curb radius and injury severity at intersections points out that "larger radii are less safe for bicycles and pedestrians because they allow for higher vehicle speeds through the turn and result in larger crossing distances."

Kendra K. Levine, *Curb Radius and Injury Severity at Intersections* (Berkeley: Institute of Transportation Studies Library, 2012), 2.

2   Research has shown that large trucks will have "little impact" at most urban intersections, but some adverse operational effects should be expected at some intersections.

Joseph E. Hummer, Charles V. Zegeer, and Fred R. Hanscom, *Effects of turns by larger trucks at urban intersections,* (Charlotte, N.C.: Transportation Academy, Dept. of Geography and Earth Sciences, University of North Carolina at Charlotte, 1988).

3   Kay Fitzpatrick and William Schneider, *Turn speeds and crashes within right-turn lanes*, (College Station, Tex: Texas Transportation Institute, Texas A&M University System, 2005).

4   In infrequent instances where large vehicles need to make turning movements, personnel may be needed to direct traffic and "spot" the turning vehicle through a tight turning movement.

5   Roadway striping has been found to be a cost-effective temporary measure to help enforce traffic calming goals and modify driver behavior.

Robert Kahn and Allison Kahn Goedecke, "Roadway striping as a traffic calming option," *ITE Journal*: 81 (September 2011).

VISIBILITY/SIGHT DISTANCE

1   Vehicle codes state that drivers must yield to drivers on the right, which necessitates slowing down.

City of Portland, Oregon, "Uncontrolled Intersections and You," accessed June 3, 2013, http://www.portlandoregon.gov/transportation/article/284482.

2   Parking is typically restricted within 10–25 feet of a crosswalk. San Francisco uses 10 feet; New Jersey adopted 25 feet within a marked or unmarked crosswalk.

New Jersey, *New Jersey statutes annotated: Title 39 :4 Motor vehicles and traffic regulation.*

FHWA Safety Program, "Remove/Restrict Parking," accessed June 3, 2013, http://safety.fhwa.dot.gov/saferjourney/library/countermeasures/56.htm.

3   San Francisco standards allow trees 25 feet from the near-side and 5 feet from the far-side curbs.

"Guidelines for Planting Street Trees," San Francisco Department of Public Works, accessed June 3, 2013, http://www.sfdpw.org/Modules/ShowDocument.aspx?documentid=622.

Elizabeth Macdonald, Alethea Harper, Jeff Williams, and Jason A. Hayter, *Street trees and Intersection Safety*, (Berkley: Institute of Urban and Regional Development, University of California at Berkeley, 2006).

4   Pedestrian scale lighting may be added to existing vehicle poles or between poles.

Complete Streets Complete Networks—A Manual for the Design of Active Transportation (Chicago: Active Transportation Policy, 2012).

Spacing depends upon existing lighting available, roadway width, and quality of lighting, but in general lighting every 50 feet provides a secure nighttime walking atmosphere.

Project for Public Spaces, "Lighting Use & Design," accessed June 3, 2013, http://www.pps.org/reference/streetlights/.

TRAFFIC SIGNALS

1   A.C. Fayish and Frank Gross, "Safety effectiveness of leading pedestrian intervals evaluated by a before–after study with comparison groups," *Transportation Research Record No. 2198* (2010): 15–22.

2   Ron Van Houten, Ralph Ellis, and Jin-Lee Kim, "Effects of Various Minimum Green Times on Percentage of Pedestrians Waiting for Midblock "Walk" Signal," *Transportation Research Record No. 2002* (2007).

3   When actuated, the direction of travel with a green phase should be given ample time to safely change from green to yellow then red. The amount of time for the yellow change interval is dependent on approach speed (presumably 25 mph or less), which would require 3 seconds. The time that should be given for the clearance interval (red signal for all legs of intersection) is dependent on the approach speed and intersection width. An approach speed of 25 mph and an intersection width of 70 feet would recommend a clearance interval of 2.5 seconds.

James A. Bonneson, Srinivasa R. Sunkari, and Michael P. Pratt, *Traffic signal operations handbook* (College Station: Texas Transportation Institute, 2009).

4   Harriet R. Smith, P. Brendon Hemily, and Miomir Ivanovic. *Transit signal priority (TSP): A Planning and Implementation Handbook* (Washington, D.C.: ITS America, 2005).

Design Controls

DESIGN CONTROLS

1   Eric Dumbaugh and Wenhao Li, "Designing for the Safety of Pedestrians, Cyclists, and Motorists in Urban Environments," *Journal of the American Planning Association.* 77:1 (2011): 69–88.

In 2010, 4,280 pedestrians were killed—an increase of 4% from 2009. Approximately 70,000 pedestrians were injured in 2010.

Traffic Safety Facts—2010 Data (Washington, D.C.: National Highway Traffic Safety Administration, 2012).

DESIGN SPEED

1   "Pedestrian Safety Review: Risk Factors and Countermeasures," (Salt Lake City: Department of City & Metropolitan Planning, University of Utah; School of Public Health and Community Development, Maseno University: 2012).

2   A. Bartmann, W. Spijkers and M. Hess, "Street Environment, Driving Speed and Field of Vision" Vision in Vehicles III (1991).

W. A. Leaf and David F. Preusser. *Literature review on vehicle travel speeds and pedestrian injuries.* (Washington, D.C.: U.S. Dept. of Transportation, National Highway Traffic Safety Administration, 1999).

Reaction plus braking distance is based on numerous factors, including the conditions of the roadway, slope, and other unique elements.

Ireland Road Safety Authority, "Stopping distances for cars," accessed June 3, 2013, www.rulesoftheroad.ie/rules-for-driving/speed-limits/speed-limits_stopping-distances-cars.html.

University of Pennsylvania School of Engineering, "Vehicle Stopping Distance and Time," accessed June 3, 2013, www.seas.upenn.edu/~ese302/lab-content/STOPPING_DISTANCE_DOC.pdf.

Driving Test Success, "Stopping Distances," accessed June 3, 2013, www.drivingtestsuccess.com/tests/stopping-distances.

3   Rosén E., and U. Sander. "Pedestrian fatality risk as a function of car impact." (*Accident; Analysis, and Prevention* 41, 2009), 536–542.

4   *Designing Walkable Urban Thoroughfares: A Context Sensitive Approach* (Washington, D.C.: Institute of Transportation Engineers, 2010), Chapter 7.

5   *Relationship Between Lane Width and Speed: Review of Relevant Literature* (Parsons Transportation Group, 2003).

DESIGN VEHICLE

1   *A Policy on Geometric Design of Highways and Streets,* (Washington, D.C.: AASHTO, 2011), Section 2-1.

2   Kendra K. Levine, *Curb Radius and Injury Severity at Intersections* (Berkeley: Institute of Transportation Studies Library, 2012).

3   Most state vehicle codes stipulate that drivers should turn right "as close as practical" to the right-hand curb or edge of the roadway. "Practical" is not defined and the code does not ban use of multiple lanes to complete a turn if needed. For example, see:

Illinois General Assembly, "625 ILCS 5/ Illinois Vehicle Code," *Illinois Compiled Statues* (Springfield).

4   Curb extensions can improve emergency vehicle access by keeping the intersection clear of parked cars.

FHWA Safety Program, "Traffic Calming," accessed June 3, 2013. http://safety.fhwa.dot.gov/saferjourney/library/countermeasures/23.htm.

Emergency vehicle codes require ambulances and fire trucks to slow down at intersections and remain alert for other users. For example, see:

Illinois General Assembly, "625 ILCS 5/ Illinois Vehicle Code, Section 11-205," in *Illinois Compiled Statues* (Springfield).

In Pennsylvania, ambulances are specifically required to comply with stop signs and red lights.

Pennsylvania Department of Motor Vehicles, "Vehicle Code—Chapter 31," (Harrisburg), 2.

Dan Burden and Paul Zykofsky. "Emergency Response: Traffic Calming and Traditional Neighborhood Streets," (Sacramento: The Local Government Commission Center for Livable Communities, 2001)

Ryan Snyder et al. "Best Practices: Emergency Access in Healthy Streets," (Los Angeles: Los Angeles County Department of Public Health, 2013).

5   Currently, many cities use SU-30 as the design vehicle on non-truck routes. For example, see:

"Design Criteria," *Seattle Right-of-Way Improvements Manual* (Seattle: City of Seattle, 2012).

6   Low "crawl" speeds are referenced by *Flexibility in Highway Design,* (Washington, D.C.: U.S. Dept. of Transportation, Federal Highway Administration, 1997).

7   In New York City, approximately 10% of pedestrian injuries occur at "off-road" locations, such as on sidewalks or inside buildings.

Transportation Alternatives, "1,200 NYC Pedestrians Struck On Sidewalks Every Year," accessed June 3, 2013, http://www.transalt.org/files/newsroom/streetbeat/askta/030425.html.

8   *City Freight Master Plan* (Portland: Portland Office of Transportation, 2006).

DESIGN HOUR

1   The phenomenon of traffic evaporation is the flip side of induced demand. When road diets occur, drivers choose an alternate route or even an alternate mode.

S. Cairns, S. Atkins, and P. Goodwin, "Disappearing traffic? The story so far," *Municipal Engineer* 151 (2001): 13–22.

2   DDOT (Washington, D.C.) *Comprehensive Transportation Review Manual* requires project applicants to collect traffic data from 7–10 AM and 4–7 PM.

DDOT Guidelines for Comprehensive Transportation Review (CTR) Requirements (Washington, D.C.: District Department of Transportation, 2012).

3   Data collected by the Pima Association of Governments.

"Annual Traffic Count Program," Pima Association of Governments, accessed June 3, 2013, http://www.pagnet.org/regionaldata/ traveldataandforecasting/annualtrafficcountprogram/ tabid/108/default.aspx.

4   DDOT's Comprehensive Transportation Review Manual states that any proposed changes to roadway geometry must not add delay to other modes. Project applicants must show how a project affects bicycle, pedestrian, and transit travel.

DDOT Guidelines for Comprehensive Transportation Review (CTR) Requirements (Washington, D.C.: District Department of Transportation, 2012).

The city of Baltimore's Traffic Impact Study guidelines require that project submissions include counts for pedestrians and cyclists as well as vehicles.

Procedures and Requirements for Conducting a Traffic Impact Study in Baltimore City Pursuant to Ordinance 06–45 (Baltimore: Baltimore City Department of Transportation, 2007).

5   An estimate of the cost of adding a lane, including new curb and sidewalk, to an urban arterial ranges from $1.65 million [*Roadway Cost Per Centerline Mile* (Tallahassee: Florida Department of Transportation, 2012).] to $4 million [*Houston's Travel Rate Improvement Program: "Toolbox" of Improvement Strategies* (College Station: Texas A&M University, 2001).].

DESIGN YEAR

1   Vehicle Miles Traveled (VMT) trends are captured by the Office of Highway Policy Information.

"Traffic Volume Trends," accessed June 3, 2013, http://www.fhwa.dot.gov/policyinformation/travel_ monitoring/tvt.cfm.

The USDOT reports that the percentage of the US population between ages 16 and 19 holding a driver license has been in decline since 1998. While some of this may be caused by increases in minimum age to drive, trends also hold true for those aged 18, 19, and into their 20s.

2   State Smart Transportation Initiative, "Motor vehicle travel demand continues long-term downward trend in 2011," accessed June 3, 2013, http://www.ssti.us/2012/02/motor-vehicle-travel- demand-continues-long-term-downward-trend-in-2011/ vmt-chart-2/.

3   Additional information on the NEPA environmental review process for transportation can be found via the USDOT.

Interim Guidance on the Application of Travel and Land Use Forecasting in NEPA (Washington, D.C.: USDOT, 2010).

The California DOT Guide for the Preparation of Traffic Impact Studies denotes that analysis scenarios should reflect traffic volumes (trip assignment) and peak LOS for the year anticipated of project completion (as compared to a 15–25 year time horizon).

Guide for the Preparation of Traffic Impact Studies (Sacramento: California Department of Transportation, 2002).

The Utah DOT specifies that the design year is based on the level of traffic impact. Projects that generate less trips (<100 ADT) need only analyze the year of completion, whereas projects that generate more trips (greater than 10,000 ADT) require a design year at the opening day of the project, five years, and twenty years.

Traffic Impact Study Requirements (Salt Lake City: Utah Department of Transportation, 2004).

4   Pavithra Parthasarathi and David Levinson, "Post Construction Evaluation of Traffic Forecast Accuracy," Transport Policy (2010): 1–16.

5   Many cities are currently establishing goals to increase non-motorized mode share. Cities include Boston, Chicago, Minneapolis, San Francisco, Portland, and others.

6   In Washington, D.C., annual growth or decrease in through traffic is to be included in traffic analysis based on historical data provided by DDOT. A DDOT Case Manager is given the final authority on projected annual growth (or decline) factors to be used in traffic analysis. *DDOT Guidelines for Comprehensive Transportation Review (CTR) Requirements* (Washington, D.C.: District Department of Transportation, 2012).

7   *National Transportation Statistics* (Washington, D.C.: USDOT Bureau of Transportation Statistics, 2013), 71.

Data derived from bicycling data for 70 largest United States cities.

League of American Bicyclists, "Bicycle Commuting Data," accessed June 3, 2013, http://www.bikeleague.org/news/acs2010.php.

8   Traffic evaporation is the counterpart to induced traffic, in which increased capacity increases demand. Desire for roads, like all economic goods, increases and decreases as supply changes. See for example:

Douglass B. Lee, Lisa A. Klein, and Gregorio Camus, "Induced traffic and induced demand," *Transportation Research Record*. No 1659 (1999): Appendix B.

9   S. Cairns, Carmen Hass-Klau, and Phil Goodwin, *Traffic Impact of Highway Capacity Reductions: Assessment of the Evidence*, (London: Landor Pub, 1998): 29.

10 S. Cairns, S. Atkins, and P. Goodwin, "Disappearing traffic? The story so far," *Municipal Engineer* 151 (2001): 13–22.

11 A literature review of several studies focused on induced demand found that between 50–100% of new roadway capacity is often absorbed by traffic within three or more years. Furthermore, the Handbook of Transportation Engineering notes that urban highway capacity expansion often fails to significantly improve travel times or speeds due to latent demand.

Todd Litman, "Generated Traffic and Induced Travel," *ITE Journal* 71 (2001): 38–47.

12 Caltrans has developed trip-generation rates for urban infill land uses in California.

Trip Generation Rates for Urban Infill Land Uses in California (Sacramento: California Department of Transportation, 2008).

Researchers at UC-Davis have developed a *Smart Growth Trip-Generation Adjustment Tool*, which provides more accurate trip forecasts for urban areas. Final Report: *California Smart-Growth Trip Generation Rates Study* (Davis, CA: University of California, 2013).

13 Transportation is second only to buildings as a source of greenhouse gas emissions, with the vast majority of transportation emissions coming from cars and trucks. Governor Patrick signed the Global Warming Solutions Act into law in 2008, and in 2010 established targets of 25 percent reduction in GHG emissions from 1990 levels by 2020 and an 80 percent reduction from 1990 levels by 2050—the most ambitious GHG emissions limits for any state in the nation.

Massachusetts Department of Transportation, "MassDOT Goal: Triple Travel by Bicycle, Transit, Walking," (October 2012) http://transportation.blog.state.ma.us/blog/2012/10/massdot-goal-triple-travel-by-bicycle-transit-walking.html.

PERFORMANCE MEASURES

1 District Office of the Deputy Mayor for Planning and Economic Development, "Great Streets," accessed June 3, 2013, http://www.dc.gov/DC/DMPED/Programs+and+Initiatives/Great+Streets.

2 *Complete Streets Chicago* (Chicago: Chicago Department of Transportation, 2013), 110–112.

3 San Francisco Planning Department, "Transportation Sustainability Program," accessed June 3, 2013, http://www.sf-planning.org/index.aspx?page=3035.

Strategic Analysis Report on Transportation System Level of Service (LOS) Methodologies (San Francisco: San Francisco County Transportation Authority, 2003).

References

Streets

NEIGHBORHOOD MAIN STREET

Burden, Dan and Peter Lagerwey. *Road Diets: Fixing the Big Roads.* Walkable Communities, Inc., 1999.

Ewing, Reid and Michael King. *Flexible Design of New Jersey's Main Streets.* New Brunswick: Voorhees Transportation Policy Institute, 1998.

Lyles, Richard W., M. Abrar Siddiqui, William C. Taylor, Bilal Z. Malik, Gregory Siviy, and Tyler Haan. *Safety and Operational Analysis of 4-lane to 3-lane Conversions (Road Diets) in Michigan.* Lansing: Michigan Department of Transportation, 2012.

McCormick, Cullen. *York Blvd: The Economics of a Road Diet.* Los Angeles: University of California Los Angeles, 2012.

Swirsky, Karen, Nils Eddy, David Olsen, Brian Rankin, Dan Burden, and Pat Kliewer. *Main Street...when a highway runs through it: A Handbook for Oregon Communities.* Portland: Oregon Department of Transportation and Oregon Department of Land Conservation and Development, 1999.

Tan, Carol H. "Going on a Road Diet." *Public Roads* 75 (2011): 1–11.

Welch, Thomas M. "The Conversion of Four-Lane Undivided Urban Roadways to Three-Lane Facilities." Paper presented at the Urban Street Symposium, TRB Circular E-C019, Dallas, Texas, June 28–30, 1999.

GREEN ALLEY

Cassidy, Arly, Josh Newell, and Jennifer Wolch. *Transforming Alleys into Green Infrastructure for Los Angeles.* Los Angeles: Center for Sustainable Cities, University of Southern California, 2008.

Chicago Department of Transportation. *The Chicago Green Alley Handbook: An Action Guide to Create a Greener, Environmentally Sustainable Chicago.* Chicago: 2010.

Nathanson, Benjamin and Danielle Emmet. *Alley Gating & Greening Toolkit.* Baltimore: Ashoka, 2008.

Street Design Elements

LANE WIDTH

Fitzpatrick, Kay, Paul J. Carlson, Mark D. Wooldridge, and Marcus A. Brewer. *Design Factors that Affect Driver Speed on Suburban Arterials.* College Station: Texas Transportation Institute, 2000.

Parsons Transportation Group. *Relationship Between Lane Width and Speed Review of Relevant Literature.* Arlington: 2003.

Potts, Ingrid B., Douglas W. Harwood, and Karen R. Richard. "Relationship of Lane Width to Safety for Urban and Suburban Arterials." Paper presented at the Transportation Research Board 86th Annual Meeting, Washington, D.C., January 21–25, 2007.

SIDEWALKS

Boodlal, Leverson. *Providing Accessible Sidewalks and Street Crossings.* Washington, D.C.: U.S. Department of Transportation, National Highway Administration, 2003.

Brownson, R. C., E. A. Baker, R. A. Housemann, L. K. Brennan, and S. J. Bacak. "Environmental and policy determinants of physical activity in the United States." *American Journal of Public Health*, 91(12), 1995–2003.

Eyler, A.A., R.C. Brownson, S.J. Bacak, and R.A. Housemann, (2003). "The epidemiology of walking for physical activity in the United States." *Medicine & Science in Sports & Exercise* (2003): 35(9), 1529–1536.

Lowbar, Kayla. "Outdoor Cafes/Widened Sidewalks." Accessed February 15, 2013. http://depts.washington.edu/open2100/Resources/2_OpenSpaceTypes/Open_Space_Types/KaylaLowberOutdoorcafes.pdf.

Sax, Christian R., Thomas H. Maze, Reginald R. Souleyrette, Neal Hawkins, and Alicia L. Carriquiry. "Optimum Urban Clear Zone Distance." *Transportation Research Record* 2195 (2010): 27–35.

VERTICAL SPEED CONTROL ELEMENTS

Burden, Dan and Paul Zykofsky. *Emergency Response: Traffic Calming and Traditional Neighborhood Streets.* Sacramento: Local Government Commission Center for Livable Communities, 2000.

City of Portland. "Impact of Traffic Calming Devices on Emergency Vehicles Report." Accessed February 2, 2012. http://www.portlandoregon.gov/transportation/article/85498.

Delaware Department of Transportation. *Delaware Traffic Calming Design Manual.* Dover: 2012.

Huang, Herman F. and Micahel J. Cynecki. "Effects of Traffic Calming Measures on Pedestrian and Motorist Behavior." *Transportation Research Record* 1705 (2000): 26–31.

Parkhill, Margaret, Rudolph Sooklall, and Geni Bahar. "Updated Guidelines for the Design and Application of Speed Humps." Paper presented at the CITE Conference, Toronto, Ontario, May 6–9, 2007.

Sacramento City Council. *Resolution No. 2008–090 Speed Hump Program Guidelines.* Sacramento: 2008.

TRANSIT STREETS

Carry, William, Eric Donnell, Zoltan Rado, Martin Hartman, and Steven Scalici. *Red Bus Lane Treatment Evaluation.* Washington, D.C.: Institute of Transportation Engineers, 2012.

Beaton, Eric B., Evan Bialostozky, Oliver Ernhofer, Theodore V. Orosz, Taylor Reiss, and Donald Yuratovac. "Designing Bus Rapid Transit Facilities for Constrained Urban Arterials: A Case Study of the Webster Avenue BRT Running Way Design Selection Process." Paper presented at the Transportation Research Board 92nd Annual Meeting, Washington, D.C., January 13–17, 2013.

Delaware Valley Regional Planning Commission. *SEPTA Bus Stop Design Guidelines*. Philadelphia: 2012.

Hillsman, Edward L., Sara J. Hendricks, and JoAnne K. Fiebe. *A Summary of Design, Policies and Operational Characteristics for Shared Bicycle/Bus Lanes*. Tallahassee: Florida Department of Transportation Research Center, 2012.

Panero, Marta, Hyeon-Shic Shin, Allen Zedrin, and Samuel Zimmerman. *Peer-to-Peer Information Exchange on Bus Rapid Transit (BRT) and Bus Priority Best Practices*. New York: Rudin Center for Transportation Policy and Management, 2012.

Sando, T. and R. Moses. *Integrating Transit Into Traditional Neighborhood Design Policies—The Influence Of Lane Width On Bus Safety*. Tallahassee: Florida Department of Transportation, 2009.

Vanasse Hangen Brustlin, Inc., Foursquare Integrated Transportation Planning, and National Bus Rapid Transit Institute. *Bus Priority Treatment Guidelines*. Washington, D.C.: National Capital Region Transportation Planning Board, 2011.

Washington Department of Transportation. "Transit Facilities," in *Design Manual*. Olympia: 2009.

Weinstein Agrawal, Asha, Todd Goldman, and Nancy Hannaford. *Shared-Use Bus Priority Lanes on City Streets: Case Studies in Design and Management*. San Jose: Mineta Transportation Institute, 2012.

Zlatkovic, Milan, Aleksandar Stevanovic, and R. M. Zahid Reza. "Effects of Queue Jumpers and Transit Signal Priority on Bus Rapid Transit." Paper presented at the Transportation Research Board 92nd Annual Meeting, Washington, D.C., January 13–17, 2013.

Interim Design Strategies

PARKLETS

Brozen, Madeline and Anastasia Loukaitou-Sideris. "Reclaiming the Right-of-Way—Best Practices for Implementing and Designing Parklets." Paper presented at the Transportation Research Board 92nd Annual Meeting, Washington, D.C., January 13–17, 2013.

Mayor's Office of Transportation and Utilities. *Philadelphia Parklet Program Guidelines*. Philadelphia: 2013.

San Francisco Planning Department. *San Francisco Parklet Manual*. San Francisco: 2013.

TEMPORARY STREET CLOSURES

The Open Streets Guide. Street Plans and Alliance for Biking & Walking, 2012.

Intersections

Caltrans, Alta Planning+Design, and Cambridge Systematics. *Complete Intersections: A Guide to Reconstructing Intersections and Interchanges for Bicyclists and Pedestrians*. Sacramento: California Department of Transportation, 2010.

NEIGHBORHOOD TRAFFIC CIRCLES

Walking Info. "Neighborhood Traffic Circles, Seattle WA." Accessed April 9, 2012. www.walkinginfo.org/pedsafe/casestudy.cfm?CS_NUM=56.

Intersection Design Elements

CROSSWALKS

Bak, Radoslaw and Mariusz Kiec. "Influence of Midblock Pedestrian Crossings on Urban Street Capacity." *Transportation Research Record* 2316 (2012): 76–83.

Boodlal, Leverson. *Providing Accessible Sidewalks and Street Crossings*. Washington, D.C.: U.S. Department of Transportation, National Highway Administration, 2003.

Branyan, George. *DC Experience with the HAWK—Hybrid Pedestrian Signal and Rectangular Rapid Flashing Beacons*. Presentation by the District Department of Transportation.

City of Boulder Transportation Division. *Pedestrian Crossing Treatment Warrants*. Boulder: 1996.

City of Boulder Transportation Division. *Pedestrian Crossing Treatment Installation Guidelines: Installation Guidelines*. Boulder: 2011.

CTC & Associates LLC and WisDOT Research & Library Unit. *HAWK Pedestrian Signals: A Survey of National Guidance, State Practice and Related Research*. Madison: Wisconsin Bureau of Highway Operations, 2010.

Fitzpatrick, Kay, Shawn Turner, Marcus Brewer, Paul Carlson, Brooke Ullman, Nada Trout, Eun Sug Park, Jeff Whitacre, Nazir Lalani, and Dominique Lord. *TCRP Report 112/NCHRP Report 562: Improving Pedestrian Safety at Unsignalized Crossings*. Washington, D.C.: Transportation Research Board, 2006.

Hunter, William W., Raghavan Srinivasan, and Carol A. Martell. *Evaluation of the Rectangular Rapid Flash Beason at a Pinellas Trail Crossing in St. Petersburg, Florida*. University of North Carolina Highway Safety Research Center, 2009.

Ragland, David R. and Meghan Fehlig Mitman. *Driver/Pedestrian Understanding and Behavior at Marked and Unmarked Crosswalks*. Berkeley: UC Berkeley Traffic Safety Center, 2007.

Yee, Bond M. *SFMTA Crosswalk Guidelines*. San Francisco: San Francisco Municipal Transportation Agency, 2012.

CURB RADII

Levine, Kendra K. *Curb Radius and Injury Severity at Intersections.* Berkeley: Institute of Transportation Studies Library, 2012.

VISIBILITY/SIGHT DISTANCE

Macdonald, Elizabeth, Alethea Harper, Jeff Williams, and Jason A. Hayter. *Street Trees and Intersection Safety.* Berkeley: Institute of Urban and Regional Development, 2006.

Design Controls

DESIGN SPEED

Ashton, S.J. and G.M. MacKay. "Some characteristics of the population who suffer trauma as pedestrians when hit by cars and some resulting implications." Accident Research Unit: Department of Transportation and Environmental Planning, University of Birmingham, England, 1979.

Bartmann, A, W. Spijkers, and M. Hess. "Street Environment, Driving Speed and Field of Vision." In *Vision in Vehicles III,* edited by A.G. Gale et al, 281–389. Amsterdam: Elsevier Science Publishers B.V., 1991.

Rosén E., J.E. Källhammer, D. Eriksson, M. Nentwich, R. Fredriksson, and K. Smith. "Pedestrian injury mitigation by autonomous braking." *Accident; Analysis and Prevention* 42 (2010): 1949–1957.

Rosén E., H. Stigson, and U. Sander. "Literature review of pedestrian fatality risk as a function of car impact." *Accident; Analysis and Prevention* 43 (2011): 25–33.

PERFORMANCE MEASURES

The following references correspond to the list of alternative performance measures on p. 166:

Dowling, Richard. *Multimodal Level of Service Analysis for Urban Streets: Users Guide, Appendix D to Contractor's Final Report for NCHRP Project 3–70.* Oakland: National Cooperative Highway Research Program, 2008.

National Research Council (U.S.). *Highway Capacity Manual.* Washington, D.C.: Transportation Research Board, National Research Council (2000): Ch. 13.

Gehl, Jan. *Cities for People.* Washington, D.C.: Island Press, 2010.

Sanders, Rebecca, Elizabeth Macdonald, and Alia Anderson. "Performance Measures for Complete, Green Streets: A Proposal for Urban Arterials in California." Paper presented at the Transportation Research Board 88th Annual Meeting, Washington, D.C., January 11–15, 2009.

Sanders, Rebecca, Elizabeth Macdonald, Alia Anderson, David R. Ragland, Jill F. Cooper. *Performance Measures for Complete, Green Streets: Initial Findings for Pedestrian Safety along a California Corridor.* Berkeley: Safe Transportation Research & Education Center, 2011.

UCLA Center for Occupational and Environmental Health. *Walkability & Pedestrian Safety in Boyle Heights Using the Pedestrian Environmental Quality Index (PEQI)* Los Angeles: University of California Los Angeles, 2013.

Sprinkle Consulting Inc. *Bicycle Level of Service Applied Model.* Tampa: 2007.

Bicycle Compatibility Index. Washington, D.C.: USDOT Federal Highway Administration.

Similar to the Pedestrian Environmental Quality Index, BEQI was developed by the San Francisco Department of Public Health: San Francisco Department of Public Health. "Bicycle Environmental Quality Index." Accessed June 3, 2013. http://www.sfphes.org/elements/24-elements/tools/102-bicycle-environmental-quality-index.

National Research Council (U.S.). *Highway Capacity Manual.* Washington, D.C.: Transportation Research Board, National Research Council (2000).

Texas Transportation Institute. *2012 Urban Mobility Report.* College Station: Texas Transportation Institute, 2012.

American Public Transportation Association. *2011 Public Transportation Fact Book.* Washington, D.C.: American Public Transportation Association, 2011.

Lindquist, Kathy, Michel Wendt, and James Holbrooks. *Transit Farebox Recovery and US and International Transit Subsidization.* Olympia: WSDOT, 2009.

AASHTO. *A Policy on Geometric Design of Highways and Streets.* Washington, D.C.: American Association of State Highway and Transportation Officials, 2011. Section 2–66.

ITE. *Designing Walkable Urban Thoroughfares: A Context Sensitive Approach.* Washington, D.C.: Institute of Transportation Engineers, 2010.

FUNCTIONAL CLASSIFICATION

Forbes, Gerry. "Urban Roadway Classification: Before the Design Begins." Paper presented at the Urban Street Symposium, TRB Circular E-C019, Dallas, Texas, June 28–30, 1999.

Marshall, Stephen, Peter Jones, and Ian Plowright. *A Framework for Classification and Assessment of Arterial Streets.* London: University of Westminster, 2004.

Additional Research References

Campbell, Richard and Margaret Wittgens. *The Business Case for Active Transportation: The Economic Benefits of Walking and Cycling.* Gloucester, ON: Go for Green, 2004.

Daniel, Janice Steven Chien, and Rachel Liu. *Effectiveness of Certain Design Solutions on Reducing Vehicle Speeds.* Newark: New Jersey Institute of Technology, 2005.

Dixon, K. K., and K. L. Wolf. Benefits and Risks of Urban Roadside Landscape: *Finding a Livable, Balanced Response.* Proceedings of the 3rd Urban Street Symposium, Seattle, Washington, June 24–27, 2007.

Dixon, Karen K., Michael Liebler, Hong Zhu, Michael P. Hunter, and Berry Mattox. *NCHRP Report 612: Safe and Aesthetic Design of Urban Roadside Treatments.* Washington, D.C.: Transportation Research Board, 2008.

Drennen, Emily. *Economic Effects of Traffic Calming on Urban Small Businesses.* San Francisco: San Francisco State University, 2003.

Dumbaugh, Eric and Wenhao Li. "Designing for the Safety of Pedestrians, Cyclists, and Motorists in Urban Environments." *Journal of the American Planning Association* 77 (2011): 69–88.

Dumbaugh, Eric. "Design of Safe Urban Roadsides: An Empirical Analysis." *Transportation Research Record* 1961 (2006): 74–82.

Dumbaugh, Eric. "Safe Streets, Livable Streets." *Journal of the American Planning Association* 71 (2005): 283–300.

Harvey, Nina, Carla Jaynes, Yennga Khuong, and Vincent Riscica. "Framework for Innovative Public Spaces." Paper presented at the Transportation Research Board 92nd Annual Meeting, Washington, D.C., January 13–17, 2013.

Laplante, John and Barbara McCann. "Complete Streets: We Can Get There from Here." *ITE Journal* (May 2008): 24–28.

Litman, Todd Alexander. "Economic Value of Walkability." *Transportation Research Record* 1828 (2003): 3–11.

Litman, Todd. *Evaluating Complete Streets: The Value of Designing Roads for Diverse Modes, Users and Activities.* Victoria: Victoria Transport Policy Institute, 2013.

Pedestrian and Bicycle Information Center. *Case Study Compendium.* 2010.

Pratt, Richard H., Herbert S. Levinson, Shawn M. Turner, and Daniel Nabors. "TCRP Report 95: Traveler Response to Transportation System Changes." Paper presented at the Transportation Research Board 91st Annual Meeting, Washington, D.C., January 22–26, 2012.

Sanders, Rebecca L. and Jill F. Cooper. "Do All Roadway Users Want the Same Things?: Results from a Roadway Design Survey of Pedestrians, Drivers, Bicyclists, and Transit Users in the Bay Area." Paper presented at the Transportation Research Board 92nd Annual Meeting, Washington, D.C., January 13–17, 2013.

Shapard, James and Mark Cole. *Do Complete Streets Cost More than Incomplete Streets?* Washington, D.C.: Transportation Research Board, 2013.

Sztabinski, Fred. *Bike Lanes, On-Street Parking and Business: A Study of Bloor Street in Toronto's Annex Neighbourhood.* Toronto: Clean Air Partnership, 2009.

Ukkusuri, Satish, Luis F. Miranda-Moreno, Gitakrishnan Ramadurai, and Jhael Isa-Tavarez. "The role of built environment on pedestrian crash frequency." *Safety Science* 50 (2012): 1141–1151.

Other Design Guides

Abu Dhabi Urban Planning Council. *Abu Dhabi Urban Street Design Manual.* Design Guidelines, Abu Dhabi: Abu Dhabi Urban Planning Council.

Charlotte Department of Transportation. *Urban Street Design Guidelines.* Design Guidelines, Charlotte: City of Charlotte, 2007.

Chicago Department of Transportation. *Complete Streets Chicago.* Design Guidelines, Chicago: Chicago Department of Transportation, 2013.

City of Atlanta. *Connect Atlanta Plan | Street Design Guidelines.* Comprehensive Transportation Plan, Atlanta: City of Atlanta, 2008.

City of Boston. *Boston Complete Streets Design Guidelines.* Design Guidelines, Boston: City of Boston, 2010.

City of Minneapolis. *Access Minneapolis.* Plan, Minneapolis: City of Minneapolis, 2008.

City of New Haven. *New Haven Complete Streets Design Manual 2010.* Design Guidelines, New Haven: City of New Haven, 2010.

City of Phoenix. *Street Planning and Design Guidelines.* Design Guidelines, Phoenix: City of Phoenix, 2009.

City of Roanoke. *Street Design Guidelines.* Design Guidelines, Roanoke: City of Roanoke, 2007.

City of Sacramento Public Works Department. *Pedestrian Safety Guidelines.* Design Guidelines, Sacramento: City of Sacramento, 2003.

City of San Diego Planning Department, MW Steele Group, Stephner Design Group. *The City of San Diego Street Design Manual.* Design Manual, San Diego: City of San Diego, 2002.

City of San Francisco. *San Francisco Better Streets Plan.* Design Guidelines, San Francisco: City of San Francisco, 2010.

City of Seattle. *Chapter 6 | Streetscape Design Guidelines.* Design Guidelines, Seattle: City of Seattle, 2012.

City of Tacoma. *Complete Streets Design Guidelines Project.* Design Guidelines, Tacoma: City of Tacoma, 2009.

City of Toronto. *Vibrant Streets | Toronto's Coordinated Street Furniture Program Design and Policy Guidelines*. Design Guidelines, Toronto: Toronto City Planning, Clean & Beautiful City Secretariat and Transportation Services, 2006.

District of Columbia Department of Transportation. *Design and Engineering Manual*. Design Guidelines, Washington, D.C.: District of Columbia Department of Transportation, 2009.

Sydney GM Urban Design and Architecture. *Street Design Guidelines for Landcom Projects*. Design Guidelines.

Gujarat Institute for Transportation & Development Policy, Environmental Planning Collaborative. *Better streets, better cities*. Design Guidelines, Gujarat: Government of Gujarat, 2011.

Institute of Transportation Engineers. *Designing Walkable Urban Thoroughfares: A Context Sensitive Approach*. Washington, D.C., 2010.

Kimley-Horn Associates, Toole Design Group, MIG. *City of Dallas Complete Streets Design Manual [Draft]*. Design Guidelines, Dallas: City of Dallas, 2012.

Knoxville Regional Transportation Planning Organization. *Complete Streets Design Guidelines*. Design Guidelines, Knoxville: Knoxville Regional Transportation Planning Organization, 2009.

Los Angeles County. *Model Design Manual for Living Streets*. Design Manual, Los Angeles: Los Angeles County, 2011.

Metro Louisville. *Complete Streets Manual*. Design Guidelines, Louisville: Metro Louisville, 2007.

Metro Regional Services. *Creating Livable Streets: Street Design Guidelines for 2040*. Portland, 1997.

Missouri Livable Streets. *Missouri Livable Streets Design Guidelines*. Design Guidelines, Missouri Livable Streets, 2011.

National Association of City Transportation Officials. *NACTO Urban Bikeway Design Guide*. Design Guidelines, NACTO, 2011.

Neighborhood Streets Project Stakeholders. *Neighborhood Street Design Guidelines*. Design Guidelines, Salem: State of Oregon, 2000.

Nelson\Nygaard and National Complete Streets Coalition. *Complete Streets Handbook*. Kansas City: Mid-America Regional Council, 2012.

New York City Department of Transportation. *Street Design Manual*. Design Guidelines, New York City: New York City Department of Transportation, 2009.

Portland Office of Transportation. *Design Guide for Public Street Improvements*. Design Guide, Portland: Portland Office of Transportation, 1993.

Portland Office of Transportation. *Portland Pedestrian Design Guide*. Design Guide, Portland : Portland Office of Transportation, 1998.

Public Works Department, City of Sacramento. *Pedestrian Safety Guidelines*. Sacramento: 2003.

San Francisco Planning Department. "Street Designs," in *Better Streets Plan*. San Francisco: 2010.

Smart Mobility, ORW, Oman Analytics. *Street Design Guidelines | Burlington Transportation Plan*. Design Guidelines, Burlington: City of Burlington.

Storrow Kinsella Associates Inc. *Multi-Modal Corridor and Public Space Design Guidelines*. Design Guidelines, Indianapolis: Indianapolis MPO, 2008.

UK Department for Transport. *Manual for Streets*. Design Guidelines, Thomas Telford Publishing, 2007.

Credits

Project Steering Committee

Joshuah Mello, A.I.C.P.
Assistant Director of Planning: Transportation
Atlanta Department of Planning and Community Development

Michele Wynn
Public Works Manager
Atlanta Department of Public Works

Gary W. Schatz, P.E., PTOE
Austin Transportation Department

Theo Ngongang
Planning Division Chief
Baltimore Department of Transportation

Vineet Gupta
Director of Policy and Planning
Boston Transportation Department

Chris Wuellner
Division of Project Development
Chicago Department of Transportation

Nathan Roseberry, P.E.
Senior Bikeways Engineer
Chicago Department of Transportation

Jeffrey Weatherford, P.E.
Deputy Director of Public Works
Houston Department of Public Works and Engineering

Carl Smitha, P.E.
Managing Engineer
Houston Department of Public Works and Engineering

Jay Kim, P.E.
Assistant General Manager
Los Angeles Department of Transportation

Don Elwood, P.E.
Director of Transportation Planning and Engineering
Minneapolis Department of Public Works

Nicholaas Peterson
Senior Project Manager
New York City Department of Transportation

Michael Flynn, A.I.C.P., LEED PA
Director, Capital Planning and Project Initiation
New York City Department of Transportation

Jamie Parks, A.I.C.P.
Senior Transportation Planner
Oakland Public Works Department

Stephen Buckley, A.I.C.P., P.E.
Director of Policy and Planning
Mayor's Office of Transportation and Utilities, Philadelphia

Ariel Ben-Amos
Senior Planner/Analyst
Mayor's Office of Transportation and Utilities, Philadelphia

Shane Silsby, P.E.
Deputy Street Transportation Director
Phoenix Streets Department

Christine Fanchi, P.E.
Transportation Engineer
Phoenix Streets Department

Peter Koonce, P.E.
Division Manager, Signals and Street Lighting Division
Portland Bureau of Transportation

Kurt Krueger
Development Review Manager
Portland Bureau of Transportation

Seleta Reynolds, A.I.C.P.
Manager, Livable Streets Division
San Francisco Municipal Transportation Agency

Susan McLaughlin, A.I.C.P., LEED AP
Transportation Planning and Urban Design Strategy Advisor
Seattle Department of Transportation

Kevin O'Neill, A.I.C.P.
Planning and Urban Design Manager
Seattle Department of Transportation

Darby Watson
Urban Design Lead
Seattle Department of Transportation

Sam Zimbabwe, LEED AP
Associate Director, Policy, Planning, and Sustainability
District Department of Transportation

Jim Sebastian, A.I.C.P.
Manager, Active Transportation Policy, Planning, and Sustainability
District Department of Transportation

Mike Goodno
Bicycle Program Specialist
District Department of Transportation

Linda Bailey
Acting Executive Director
National Association of City Transportation Officials

David Vega-Barachowitz
Director, Designing Cities
National Association of City Transportation Officials

Consulting Team

NELSON\NYGAARD CONSULTING ASSOCIATES

Michael King, R.A. (project manager)

Stephanie Wright, A.I.C.P. (deputy project manager)

Paul Supawanich, A.I.C.P.

Will Sherman

Technical Reviewers: Chester (Rick) Chellman, P.E., Paul Moore, P.E., Michael Moule, P.E.

Interns: Sam Frommer; Alyssa Pichardo

PURE+APPLIED

Urshula Barbour

Paul Carlos

Nick Cesare

Karilyn Johanesen

Carrie Kawamura

SHERWOOD DESIGN ENGINEERS

Tom Bacus, P.E.

Theodore C. Lim, LEED AP, BD+C

BLINKTAG WEB DEVELOPMENT

Brendan Nee

Trucy Phan

Graphic renderings by Frances Hsia, National Association of City Transportation Officials

Case Studies compiled by Corinne Kisner, National Association of City Transportation Officials

SPECIAL THANKS TO

NYC DOT: Joshua Benson, Carly Clark, Thomas Maguire, David Moidel, Margaret Newman, Jon Orcutt, Sean Quinn, Matthew Roe, Ryan Russo, Bruce Schaller, Lacy Shelby, Karin Sommer, Randy Wade, Emily Weidenhof, Andy Wiley-Schwartz; Ron Thaniel, NACTO; Neil Kopper, Austin Department of Public Works; Katherine Watkins, City of Cambridge Department of Public Works; Romel Pascual, City of Los Angeles; Stephen Villavaso, CicLAvia

Photo Credits: NYC DOT; University City District, Philadelphia; Michael King, Nelson\Nygaard Consulting Associates; David Vega-Barachowitz, NACTO; Michael Flynn, NYC DOT; Joshua Mello, City of Atlanta; Susan McLaughlin, Seattle DOT; Ariel Ben-Amos, City of Philadelphia; Olugbenro Ogunsemore; GREENGARAGE; Sherwood Engineers; Paul Supawanich